BREADCRUMBS, VOL. 2

BREADCRUMBS, VOL. 2
POEMS & PROSE
FOUND ALONG THE SACRED PATH

JAMES ANTHONY ELLIS

For permissions please contact:
James Anthony Ellis
E-mail: JimEllis1103@gmail.com

Breadcrumbs, Vol. 2 Poems & Prose Found Along the Sacred Path
Published by:
Legacy Productions
LegacyProductions.org

Library of Congress Control Number: 2024902252
ISBN 979-8-218-35028-4

Book Design and Cover by Olga Singer of SimplyTwo Design
Cover Photo secured by Legacy Productions
Copyright language: English

Printed by Ingram Spark, Publishers Group West
Berkeley, California USA

First Edition: February 2024

Dedicated to
the original state of purity, the darkness, the falling, the rising,
the growth, and the path of light that will lead us all back home.

Contents

FOREWORD

I met Jim Ellis in 2003 when I joined an international men's organization called Mentor, Discover, Inspire (MDI). He has been a teammate and close friend ever since.

Over the years, I have hired Jim to create Poetry Portraits for several of my family members. The first poem he did for me was for my mom as a gift on Mother's Day 2014. Called *Always There*, the prose told of how my mother has been there for me throughout my entire life. He interviewed me about my mom then turned that into the most beautiful poem I had ever heard. To this day, I cannot read it without crying. My mom was so touched it brought her to tears as well.

Since then, Jim has written four more poems for me:

1. One for my dad called *These Make the Man*, one in which he read at my father's funeral in 2022.

2. One for a close friend Russ, who passed in 2014, called *He was a Fighter*, also read by Jim at Russ' celebration of life.

3. A poem for my daughter after she reached a long-term dream of becoming a court reporter. It was called, *Yes, Yes – I Can Do This*.

4. One very touching and well-received poem for a girlfriend.

At one point for my birthday in September 2020, I was surprised to receive my own Poetry Portrait called, *Living a Life of Gratitude*. It has been my most prized possession.

Two of these poems I mentioned are included in this book.

Having Jim read my father's poem at his funeral was such an honor. Jim totally nailed it – the man my dad was to me, to my brother and to everyone in the room. It capped off a beautiful service.

I am amazed how Jim can interview someone and turn it into a piece of art. His poems for my loved ones make such thoughtful and caring gifts. These are sentiments directly from my heart, put into such a wonderful form. He can take my feelings and put them onto paper so beautifully. That is why I keep having Jim write these for me.

Jim has been a part of so many aspects of my life. From friend to mentor to amazing poet to videographer at my daughter Marissa's wedding. He has shown up so strong and powerfully each step of the way.

Now, Jim Ellis has collected 108 of his most moving pieces, with the deep love and care oozing from every word. You will be gifted by reading *Breadcrumbs* so you too can experience what he puts into his sacred writing.

Willy Holt
October 2023

Preparing for the Journey – An Introduction

I started this journey so long ago. What? Like 60 years ago?

My first poem I recall writing, and then memorizing, was written at age 10. Titled *The Clock of my Life*, it reflected on the awareness of time and the importance of spending it wisely. Age 10? That poem actually made it as the first poem in my first volume of poetry, *Breadcrumbs: Poems & Prose Designed to Lead You Home*, published in 2012.

Over the decade since that publication, I have been one busy rhymer guy. I didn't notice the time going by or how prolific I had been over the years. In the summer of 2023, after I finally chose to gather up all the pieces of prose, I saw that I had written over 275 poems. Wow.

I figured it was time.

This second volume of poetry is called *Breadcrumbs: Poems & Prose Found Along the Sacred Path*. I noticed that so many of these poems were dedicated to a spiritual journey, an awakening in mind, body, and spirit, as well as a shift from unconsciousness and darkness to awareness and light. Therefore, the decision was made to sift through them all, locate the 108 that best told the story from beginning to end, and present that journey to you. Once again – as found in the Hansel and Gretel fairy tale – the analogy here is that I shall leave behind breadcrumbs along the path so there is a clear way back … hoping the birds don't get to the clues first.

These 108 pieces of sacred prose, sectioned off into 11 sub-themes, are ready for your consumption at the pace that best suits your own journey.

I include in this book a selection of six *Poetry Portraits*, which are poems sculpted from the words of someone giving a gift of poetry to a loved one. For these poems, I would sit with a client, interview him or her about a loved one and then sculpt a rhyming poem, like a piece of art or a painted portrait. Over the years I have received such overwhelming positive responses to this service. One mother who received a poem from her two young children told me that she has read that piece every single night before going to bed for the past seven years. It is within these pages called *Always*. I hope, though the portraits found in chapter 12 may not speak directly to your life experiences, they speak directly to your own heart – the whole intention of all these poems.

Here in this book, may your heart be touched, may your mind be opened, may you find yourself on your own sacred voyage, heading to a home you never forgot and one in which you will celebrate upon your arrival.

With 60 years of life experience, a decade of writing and rhyming, traveling with this "clock of my life" – all done so that I may share the journey with you. Enjoy.

James Anthony Ellis
October 2023

A Perfect Place to Start

Here we go…

Here we begin our journey. This is the starting point, that place of purity, excitement and anticipation before the soul moves along into the world of duality. Though such a world may tear at the soul through tough and tragic life experiences, that primordial state is never truly lost forever.

Even though veils of delusion may cover us, due to our pains and our losses, we still maintain a perfect place within, a beauty beyond compare. So why must the soul traverse through such harsh experiences in an all-too-often cruel world?

I guess we are to find out … on this journey.

Come To Me And Be With Me

Sometimes when I need inspiration,
I just surrender to the sweet will of that which has always been faithful to me.

Come to me and be with me
Let me see what you can see
And fly with feathers on ocean breeze
Ache no more ... in a life with ease
I bow to you, on bended knees
Begging please, oh pretty please
That I can see what you can see
Oh come to me and be with me

Come to me this very day
Let me hear what you will say
I want to listen, I want to heed
I anguish, I suffer, I stretch, I bleed
For what I want, for all I need
Fertile ground cries for sacred seed
I beseech, I beg, I pray, I plead
Let me hear what you will say
Come to me this very day

Come to me my hallowed muse
It's you I never wish to lose
An instrument of God, I'm here to use
Come to me my hallowed muse
Come to me and be with me
Let me see what you can see
Let me hear what you can say
Let me live in moments of today
Let me cry out for the truths of truth
Let me rest in eternal proof

Let me write what comes from above
Let me write what comes from love
Let me channel all that is good and divine
Let me know what truly is mine
I bow to you, on bended knees
Begging please, oh pretty please
That I will be what you will be
Angels, spirit, light ... oh come to me and be with me

A BEAUTY BEYOND COMPARE

Today, I marvel at the vision before me.
A youngster – a mere 2 and 1/2 year old.
I write this one with a heart weary of the bad news of the day.
That can be kept at bay.
For today, here is a grand opportunity to see beyond the dark edges brought
to us by a world which has forgotten its source.
Here is my chance.
A simple glance – upon this illumined face, the deep round eyes, holding
not one hint of disguise. The pure expression, filled with the unbridled joy
of brand-new exploration.
Here is Abigail.
Holding her Abby Doll.
Apparently inseparable, at least in images in recent memory.
Here is Abigail, my niece's child.
Sister of Allison – also new to this new world.
May her light, may their light, guide the way. Not just for themselves,
but for anyone who has the opportunity to join in this experience,
a chance at a glance – captured in a photo I wish to share.
A beauty beyond compare.

ALL THINGS GREAT

A poem and prayer at Christmastime 2018 for my wife Jennifer. These are moments when the glass is half full, and life is all about the celebration.

And so we continue this crazy game
The prayer, as always, remains the same
In all things great, our abundance is ours
From the grains of sand to the faraway stars
From the dawn of light to the fading night
From our surrender to God to fighting the good fight
From the lows of lows to the highs of highs
From the flower in the walkway to the heavenly skies
From the love of consideration to the rage of disrespect
From the doubt and dread to the needs that are met
Our father in heaven guarding over a little girl and boy
Our prayer: our health and wealth and joy

Yes, all things great – they belong to us
As long as we align with love and trust
As long as we remember what is truly real
As long as we're willing to deeply reveal
As long as we – even in darkness – still believe
In the sacred light … we still can perceive
As long as we process the angst, judgment and hate
Here, in harmony, we embrace all things great

So this prayer is made; the intention is set
In patience, we know God's promises are kept
Though troubles may come and times may get tough
The Dolphins may lose, and the Kings may suck
Through mortgage mayhem and through bills that mount
It's beauty and grace and miracles that count

The gifts of a life where we love and laugh
The high fives when we score are always a blast
The quaint walks and talks in the parks' sunlight
The Venti hot chocolates if they ever get it right
The oatmeal and blueberries and eggs that are free
Perfect, as always, our elegant pooch Hennessy
Striving for a life of freedom, fairness, peace and liberty
The work – though at times maddening – that creates legacy
And all that is left, the splendor that is our fate
As we proclaim, in full abundance, all that is great

THE FAITHFUL MUSE

I may say I want to be left alone at times, but when it comes to needing inspiration,
I welcome the muse, no matter how pushy and demanding she can be.

Oh my goodness – your voice, your encouragement, it beckons
And geez, sitting my butt in my chair is a good idea, I reckon
But there are 1001 distractions that keep knocking at me
Organize the pencil drawer, eat a cupcake, climb a tree
Answer another e-mail, gotta empty that inbox you know
Woops – here comes some more e-mail, only 5 more now to go
Clean off the desk completely, maybe use microfiber on the screen
Must make sure before I start writing that everything is clean
Clean and clear, everything in its place, nothing to erase
So that when I am ready, I can convene sweetly face to face
With the guiding presence that delivers a gift that I cannot lose
Life is grand with the nagging inspiration of the agitating muse

The agitating muse – OK, OK, I can hear you screaming my name
Whenever it is time to channel your words, it's always the same
I get annoyed with every tasky task that is put upon my plate
I wince in pain, fidget in my chair, find creative ways to hesitate
I feel like my body is moving in one direction and it's all wrong
I want to be faithful to the lilting voice echoing a serene song
But I got all this crap to do, not even sure what it's all for
My left brain and right brain are in an all-out war
When it gets this crazy, I feel this aggravation and agitation
I long for the action that comes from pure motivation
I gotta find a way out of this conflict or I will blow a fuse
If only all I had to heed was the nagging inspiration of
the agitating muse

Perhaps there is a way, a path, an opening, a road of real recovery
Leading to a clearing in a field we share, a place of deep discovery
Where chaos can reign and rule over the outside world of the blind
Noticed, acknowledged, accepted, but not followed by a wandering mind
Here – sitting calm, with a centered and still body is best, I reckon
Oh my goodness – your voice, your encouragement, it beckons
And yes it is actually beautiful, not agitating at all, when I listen clearly
It only wants to hold high a vision; it only wants to hold me dearly
And whisper its wonder through inspirational pictures and lyrical tone
Reminding me that at the deepest core, I am never alone
Let the e-mails pile up, let the desktop get cluttered,
there is only one thing to do
I am here, with my partner in prose – the astonishing, generous,
faithful muse

HERE'S TO YOU, DEAR SEARCHER

The journey began a long time ago for all searchers who will ultimately find what he or she is looking for. I think it's one of those universal guarantees.

We come to this space of unconditional love
Seeking to find what is below and what is above
Opening our minds and opening our hearts
To return once again to that brand new start

It begins with surrender, and then a deep breath
A rebirth into bliss, to a life beyond death
Into the timeless, the spaceless, into the sweet will
Where thoughts cease fire, and deep waters run still

Here's to you, dear searcher – you'll find your way home
Where there is the one reality, where you're never alone
We dive within ourselves, to discover that pure gold
The innocence that is our birthright, a love story to be told

So, celebrate today and always, be here and now
Traveling as far as you wish, to where your safety will allow
We acknowledge all you've done, and all there is to do
As you discover the meaning, and the truth of the real you

Here's to you, dear searcher – planting seeds to be sown
Realizing your true nature, finding your own pathway home

Leaving the Harbor

This piece was written for the opening ceremony of an international conference dedicated to eradicating abuse and trauma on the planet. I imagine we have to start somewhere. And so — with a destination in mind — we do.

And so we begin our journey
All of us here – in this room and beyond
We leave the harbor behind
Waving goodbye, the port is now gone

We have christened this ship
We have pulled anchor from the sea
We have set out our sail
It carries us all – you and me
Sailing on to a dream
To a land we'll call "Avalon"
A place of peace, harmony and hope
It beckons us, on and on
Ending the nightmare
Of violence, abuse and trauma
Working together to soothe the sores
Dropping the curtain on this drama

Yes, we start out on our journey
All of us here – in this room and beyond
We leave the harbor behind
Waving goodbye, the port is now gone

But what lay ahead is a dream, a hope
A home, a haven, a land
A sure footing on the slippery slope
A peace that we can understand

Beyond the silence and the shame
Beyond the violence and crushed voices
Beyond the bitterness and the blame
To a high haven of infinite choices

As we set out for this gentle place
It beckons us, on and on
It calls to us, like a friendly face
To the shores of Avalon
The shores of Avalon

The Fall
Struggles and Challenges

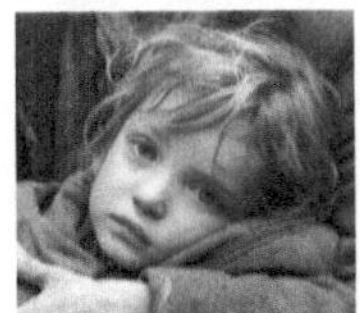

Along our journey, we may bump up against a few struggles, challenges, and barriers. You know – life. The hard stuff.

The losses, the pain, the breakups, the delusions, the let downs. All those places that can trigger the emotional spiral into fear … and worse.

Heck, since it's part of the journey, let's grab a special vantage point and observe these darker moments that make up the full breadth of a life worth living.

SOMEBODY'S BABY

*A poem inspired by a walk downtown where I saw a homeless woman
I will most likely never see again.*

I walked our regular daily walk today
Seeing the routine views along the way
Trees and streets, and then skies up there
I observe the sights – I breathe the air
Then quickly something catches my attention
Shaking my head, I grasp for comprehension
A troubled one – limping, dirty, disheveled – a lonely and lost lady
Once upon a time, that was somebody's baby

That was the phrase that flashed across my mind
Too late, to now turn my head away, blind
Where is she going, where did she come from
Too easy to throw her aside like some runaway bum
No, this one, like all of us, has a history and a life
She has had very similar battles, struggles and fights

Perhaps cradled, as an infant, in warm arms – maybe?
The truth is, that was indeed somebody's baby

Who does this soul belong to, an angel she must have
Someone who watches over her, even with the past she's had
Whatever happened, there was at least a father and a mother
For how long this lasted, we will probably never discover
But she is a human – once and therefor forever one of us
Embracing her in some way, a true and faithful community must
Someday to reside in a sacred place – calm, serene, shady
For this is somebody's baby ... this is somebody's baby

THE INVISIBLE SCAR

A piece of poetry about the scars we cannot see, but ones that impact us still.

Where do we look, when observing the scars of life
A scratch from our dog, a puncture wound from kitchen knife
A skateboard accident, it threw you five feet high
It's not what you meant, communication gone awry
A hurtful word, spoken in an angry moment's heat
An addiction habit that you can't help but repeat
A surgery's reminder that a doctor visited here
A child's neglect, abuse, molest, terror and fear
From the dent deep, a fender bender on a favorite car
To the unsettling sleep, whispering a subconscious, silent scar

Scars I cannot feel
Scars I cannot see
Scars I cannot heal
Scars that are a part of me

And so, even in dismay, we make a path our way
Traversing through the troubles of the day
Bruised in the battles, bones and egos broken
We search for salve, that truth to be spoken
The mirror reflects the ugliness directly back at us
When we lose face, lose faith, lose the will to trust
Yet persevere we must, holding onto Sun behind cloud
Seeking the higher reflection, the angel's voice crying loud
Hearing the song of the soul that, at once, we can embrace
Leaving us still, in surrendered will, in the glory of our grace
Yes, as you arrive, fully alive, you'll see it was never far
Guided on, all along, behind the sacred, silent scar

Scars that show you what to feel
Scars that see you through
Scars that love will ultimately heal
Scars that are not you

THE GREAT MOTIVATOR

*So, what moves us on our chosen path? It can be different for each person.
I know at least one motivator that moves us all, whether we think we are ready
to move or not …*

Yes, oh yes, the great motivator
The great motivator
It is here; it is now
Ringing its triumphant bell, calling out its clarion call
Never to be denied, always to be heard
It is here, now: the great motivator
It moves us all from here to there
It strikes a chord, encouraging us to share

So deep, so deep, so deep

It is here; it is now
The great motivator

Never to be denied, never to allow any one of us to hide
Convincing us to climb for the highest goals
Tearing down the phony–baloney roles
Reinstating the lonely and searching souls

It is here; it is now

Never to be denied
Never allowing one to hide
Blowing apart separation and sides
Collapsing time frames, forcing skulls to collide
With a rush and a push and a triumphant lift from inside

Always to be there in case we fall prey
Falling to the side as we make our straying way

Through forests of shadows that promise to betray
No longer allowing avoidance, resistance or delay

Ah yes, the great motivator

Pain, pain
Ah yes, pain

The great, great motivator

Our Cozy Little Hideaway

Along our journey, we all may want a hiding place away from the pain and the darkness. Yet, where do we go when we've run out of hiding places?

The fan is hit – by you know what
The joke is funny and you're the butt
The jig is up, the targets on you
You search your mind for what to do
You must escape; you must hide your head
You must have others consider others instead
What to do, where to go
You know, this joint ... you want to blow
So run and hide, run away
To your cozy little hideaway
Your cozy little hideaway

Criticism raises its crooked finger
Shame and pain find ways to linger
You're accountable to accounting right
The wrongness is what you have to fight
And fight you will – to the bitter end
Until every action you must defend
Stand and deliver your territory side
Until it becomes your place to hide
A fortress armed with canon, grenade and gun
Protecting only you and serving no one
Like shadows at the end of the day
Soon you will have nothing more to say
In your cozy little hideaway
Your cozy little hideaway

A cozy little haven with no one around
Safe and sound, safe and sound

No one to judge you, critique you, see you
No one to harm you, know you ... be you
A cozy little sanctuary, serenity found
Safe and sound, safe and sound

Though some may miss it and some may curse it
The loss of humanity will somehow be worth it
Your loss happened long ago, before this poem
When you happened to notice, you were all alone
Your hurt led you inward, your pain led you here
To that dwelling where you could disappear
Wounded by cuts, grades A through F
Proving once more, you were not the best
Failures and forced speeches, scantrons and curves
Getting not what you wanted but what you deserve
An echo of agony down the classroom history hall
Picked on at school, or picked last for basketball
Running scared, running blind, running rogue
Comparisons come by way of Cosmo and Vogue
Comparisons come by way of the final score
Or when you're abruptly shown the other side of the door

Now you're out of tune in your own sad song
Now you're ruined by a need to be right and not wrong
Now you can't say you're sorry, and can't apologize
Can't distinguish the profane, the sacred, the wicked or the wise
Can't honor your commitments, or stand by your word
And anyone who notices is labeled absurd
And anyone who says so is said to be obscene
And anyone who points it out is claimed to be mean
You have constructed your own shield from grievances and consideration
Can't be burdened by all this consternation
You validate avoidance and living without care
Claiming in your own reality, everything is fair
You justify ignoring the mail, the messages and phone
You're OK with leaving all these people alone

Until you find yourself nowhere, where you rightfully belong
No friends can reach you, and family is gone
Here you would rather lay down and die
Than be humble, vulnerable or surrender to the sky
Never to venture out, never to dare
This is a place we arrive, and finally share
Nestled there in the forest of fear and decay
Our cozy little hideaway
Our cozy little hideaway

LEVERAGE

*I got in touch at one point with what I consider the underlying dark force
ruining our relationships. Do you see what I see? Over the years people have used
leverage over others in a way most detrimental to a unity that could save them.
Once you see it, you can't unsee it.*

Meet the real evil
The real deal
The offer you just can't pass up
What a set up
You and another
With one over the other
Refusing defeat
You must rinse and repeat
Over and over
Getting the upper hand
Getting them under your thumb
Don't look stupid, don't look dumb
You are the one!
To have won...
The battle, the court case, the game, the match, the conversation,
the relationship
All you need is not love
But rather leverage
Leverage over the other
Be it sister, brother, father, sibling, lover
Everyone run for cover
For someone must win so the other must lose
For someone must manipulate, control and confuse
Muggers with and without guns
But perhaps a majority of the funds
Mortgages and banks hold the key to your account

As they count hundreds as you count pennies
Overdraft fees in cascading degrees
As their mistakes come with only apologies
Cheaters make sure to wield the advantage
Predicting balls and strikes with machinery
The trickery
Found everywhere ... where life is unfair
Lawyers in the best-baloney competition
Political lobbyist polishing the best smile
All the while ...
Man physically overpowers woman
Woman strategically overpowers man
It's the same freaking plan
When you come to understand
When you see the real deal
As you meet face to face
In the hell of separation
In the pit of disgrace
Meeting finally
The real evil ...
Leverage

CRUSH THE FLOWER

Have you ever had a partner, lover, friend who constantly sees the glass as half-empty? It sure can be a bummer. It sure can mask what's really going on.

Destroy me with your mind
Carve me ugly, cut unkind
Paint me colors dark and gray
Be disturbed by all my ways
Leave the love, let it sour
And crumple, crumple, crush the flower

Make me a puppet for your feelings
Whose source must go unknown, unnamed
Prop me up as a cardboard cutout
For you to mock, defile and blame

See not the darkness that springs your hate
See not the emptiness that seals our fate
See not the voice that cries in pain
See not a heart that sings in vain

But see the agitating stains on clothes
And thorns on every sentimental rose
And see the socks – they do not match
And criticize with a crooked finger scratch
And do not see the beauty, the power
But crumple, crumble, crush the flower

See not the darkness that springs your hate
See not the emptiness that seals our fate
See not the voice that cries in pain
See not a heart that sings in vain

Egos, Tyrants and Kings

*There is a beautiful world when dear ones receive our calls and return a
message in kind. And then there are other experiences not so much. T
his poem was inspired by those friends and loved ones who selectively bypass a
chance to return a message or respond to an outstretched hand.
I mean admit it — that avoidance can't come from a good place.
After realizing that, the prose took off from there.*

At the end of the day, when all has been said
There will be the will of the living, and memories of the dead
There will be times of consideration by those who truly cared
There will be blankets and cookies and treasures that were shared
There will be sacrifices made by parents for their young
There will heroes who embraced the good for everyone
And then yet, there will be culprits whose hubris overruled everything
Watch out for the egos, tyrants and kings

They arrive in the night and take just for themselves
They'll drown out common courtesy with whistles and bells
Their conversations leave you invisible; it's all about them
What they've done, what they believe, and where they have been
They'll interrupt you as you speak, in the middle of your speech
They play the game of avoidance, a desperate hide and seek
You are just a meaningless prop, and they are everything
Beware of the egos, tyrants and kings

The appearance is shifty; they take many forms
They dismantle etiquette, standards and norms
Life is all on their terms; they get their own way
Agreements, contracts, commitments destroyed ... no matter what you say
At times their influence is subtle, at first the impact is slight
Though one thing is settled ... they are always right

They need not call you back; they pick and choose what to do
Unless they need something, then it's "Hey, how are you?"
Responses to pleas for help, they weigh it in their mind
They hold leverage over what's meek, gentle and kind
Amidst this self-absorption, there is no care, no hope
It's only a matter of time before the cutting becomes cutthroat
They are the snake that bites, the scorpion that stings
They are the underbelly – the egos, tyrants and kings

But in our power of choice, we can send them on their way
There will be nothing to explain, nothing to say
They've taught us a lesson, a high vision to keep
Reflecting back our own way we played hide and seek
We crouched behind their reign so we could all play so small
And avoid what would be a higher self and its caring call
Controlling, limiting and censuring ourselves all this time
Degrading, disrespecting, devaluing our precious higher mind
So with no make wrong, but only make right, we take a new stand
To be who we really are, and do all that we can
To embrace that inner culprit, he knew not what he did
He found his own way to keep it all hid
But now ushering everyone, and everything, out into the light
A brand new horizon is clearly in sight
The dove takes to the skies, the angel siren sings
God bless the egos, tyrants and kings

The Beast

There are common phrases to explain a concept: "Resist ye not evil" or "Don't feed the beast." The idea is to not engage with darkness or feed into lowly desires and activities that would only make such lower natures more powerful. Picture the angel on one shoulder whispering sage and wise advice … and then picture the other shoulder's resident…

You don't know his image, you don't know his name
Yet he influences your life … just the same
He broadcasts TV news, and songs from the devil's muse
Yet he will promise safety and comfort – that is the ruse
He undertakes clandestine deeds, from sunset to sunrise
You share some common views … that is the surprise
He resides in the outer world, creating madness and mayhem
He reflects the mirror of inner worlds – in every woman and man
You have known of the legacy, you surely know the folklore
The beast is always hungry; the beast needs more
And more

The beast needs to consume every day and every night
The beast needs to ground every heavenly flight
The beast needs to sear every ear, and blind all eyes
The beast thirsts for the blood on the battlefield of lies
The beast is your friend right up until the end of time
Until he takes everything that is yours, ours, and mine
The beast sits in waiting behind every darkened door
The beast is always hungry; the beast needs more
More and more

And where is this hunger satisfied and how is he fed?
Be astonished, the source rests upon your bedfellow's bed
Like sugar for cancer, he eats treats for sweet diseases
Like water damage in hidden crevice, he does as he pleases

Your anger is his appetizer, it garners his fine favor
Your addictions to gluttony, booze and blow he loves to savor
Revenge, suppression, and enmity help fulfill his demands
Procrastination and pity call out for idle hands
Just as theft and taxes feed the famished government machine
Just as false prophets soil the sacred into the obscene
Just as flies venture into spider webs only to be caught
We must awaken to the folly of the dance that must stop
Must stop!

The beast has needed to consume every day and every night
The beast has desired to ground every heavenly flight
Yet, the beast collapses, defeated, when abandoned on distant shore
The beast will not be hungry when there is nothing more
The beast will succumb — left deaf, blind and dumb
When you stop in your tracks, and choose … to cease to run
The beast will starve when he is no longer provided his share
Poisoned by the illumination that comes from your self-care
Lick the wound, heal the heart, unite in light, soothe the sore
And then study war, draw swords, and feed the beast no more
No more
No more

The Dark Night of the Soul

We all go through it. The question is: "How are we going to get through it?"

This night is not my night
It belongs to the realm of the hidden, out of sight
Where ghosts and shadows catapult into flight
Turning faces away from that which is right
This night is not my night

They call it the dark night of the soul
Where somehow we are to understand our role
Collapsing within, into one tight fold
Nothing left to grasp, nothing to hold
Just darkness in the dark night of the soul

So where are we to go and what are we to do?
When everything that is old removes what is new
Where everything that is false takes over the true
When everything glowing gold turns deep black and blue
Who is there to be; what is there to do?

The dark night is here; are we to fear?
Or allow it to consume all that is dear
Then devour us over time as we simply disappear
Dissolving into puddles made of 1000 tears
What are we to heed; what is left to hear?

In this, a night that must become my night
As I embrace a realm of the hidden, barely out of sight
Where shadows shatter silence in a knockdown fight
Turning all away from that which is right
This is a night that must be seen as my night
Though I share it with the angels who escape into flight
And usher in the arrival of the clarity light

Leaving dust, and brokenness in a final good night
Leaving behind the dark night that is no longer my night

32

The Darkness Trembles

I do appreciate the founding principles of the United States and the Constitutional Republic that keeps us all equal and free. I observe local and national politics, and I must say it's a scary day when darkness arises. Likewise, it's a day to celebrate when it is put in its rightful place.

Corruption arises, dark steam from underground
The wicked wield power in games of lost and found
No longer dollars sought, for they have all that they need
This goes beyond lust and hunger, games, toys and greed
The ultimate desire, undisclosed treacherous goals
The accumulation of property, destinies, and souls
Special treatment lifts egos and kings high upon its shoulders
The hypnotized blindly follow the evil mind-controllers
The cohesive comply, we may never see what reality resembles
Somewhere though, somehow … the darkness trembles
Yes indeed, somewhere somehow … the darkness trembles

Now what can we believe here, who is the taker and the giver?
Media is on the airwaves, selling everyone down the river
Blatant falsehoods – now a parade of the vicious and the sick
Politicians lies are now the latest Jedi mind-trick
Up is down, war is peace, just as many once prophesized
The glimmering glow of the show keep viewers mesmerized
Taking orders from those whose powers are meant to be limited
Masked and vaxxed citizens, now timid, controlled, inhibited
The confused need to question, so we may see what reality resembles
Somewhere, somehow the truth is … the darkness trembles
Yes indeed, somehow somewhere … the darkness trembles

But how could darkness tremble, it holds the might and power
It hides in cracks and crevices, and in the top of terror's tower

The beams of death rays have the weak bow and the fearful cower
A passport to hell, an injection of forced will, a chemtrail shower
So how can it be, in the land of the brave and the home of the free
How can we reclaim what was gifted us, from sea to shining sea?
Gifted not from man or tyrants whose hubris will have them fall
But from Divine Providence, the Creator, the overseer of all
Evil in the dark of night laughs at everyone falling for its game
Yet truth, like a rose, will stand in certainty, by any other name
The slumbering will seek to know, so all can see what reality resembles
Somewhere, somehow in anticipation … the darkness trembles
Yes indeed, seen upon horizon … the darkness trembles

In the depths, the will of "we the people" shall restore a foundation true
And the sins and sorrows and shame will gently be washed anew
Flowers will bloom, seeds will spout, the Sun shall shine its magnificent rays
The truth cannot be mocked, in the beginning, and in the end of days
A revolution of the heart, a revelation in the mind
Joining brother, sister, father and mother … in kind
The nightmare will cease, bringing a predicted peace,
so that all can truly find
What can be embraced in the moment, and what horrors can be left behind
The awakened will finalize come to know, seeing all that reality resembles
In glorious triumphant exaltation … the darkness trembles
Yes, when facing directly into the light of the Lord … the darkness trembles
The darkness trembles

WOUNDED

*None of us appear to be getting out of here without a few cuts and bruises. And
yet, there is hope.*

Wounded … wounded
Taken down
To the ground
On battlefield lying face up
Clouds form images through swollen eyes
Bows and arrows, gun barrels and smoke, violent

I am a man
Alone
Haven fallen
To the ground
Taken down
Wounded

Battle mates are strewn like litter
Battle mates abandon my carcass – for enemy birds to pick at
And devour
For I am wounded

I wish only to arise from this field
And strike again
Any foe
Any man
Anyone
All walking sticks become my target

Holding my weapon, drenched with sweat
Still hunching, still hiding behind doorways, still slithering like snake
Through burned out sheds and warehouses
In this hell

I only want to strike
Strike back
Attack
It's all I have left
In my state of mind
Wounded
I search the door latch
The escape hatch
The way out of this battle
Bombs detonating in distant caverns of my mind
The excruciating silent sound
Black hawk down
Desperate for brothers in arms to lift me up

Rope dangling above my reach
I run through jungle, over plants, through trees
Falling on my face, then up on my knees
I get up and keep running and running
And running and running
Away from ghosts with insatiable appetite nipping at my heels
Towards a line that can lift me to aircraft, home-bound
Running and running
Reaching and reaching
Until finally, finally, finally …

A comrade
A comrade grasping me – not to abuse or use, this time
But to raise me up to safe quarters – on board
Airlifted out
In skies that still hold the cloudy images – violent and vile
Yet seen from a different vantage point
Through atmosphere found gentle at this altitude
I fly

Like eagle soaring to find higher perch
Like phoenix whose ashes are a mere faint memory

I fly
Not alone
A man
Once wounded
On the ground
Left for dead
Now I fly
I fly not alone
And I fly
Home

AND SO I PRAY

When it gets so dark, sometimes all there is left to do is to pray, bringing the sacred to our earthly experiences.

On the surface we may suffer, as we ride the wild rides
Falling and scraping our knees, in the playgrounds outside
The fragile frames fight gravity, from the cradle to the grave
The body can be the home of the free and the brave
And yet tragedy can strike it down with one fatal blow
As we push and pull our way along the pathways we go
Disease and viruses can attack, and force decay
And so I pause … and so I pray

Relationships continue the glory of the wicked unknown
Revealing secrets about ourselves even we had not known
There is he and she and then me and we
Pushing us beyond barriers, so we can be who we can be
Discovering new hearts, new eyes, open to see
Uncovering the truths that shall set us free
But first we may walk through darkness, as we fight, separate, betray
And so I pause … and so I pray

Communities, societies, nations hold hushed destinies
Broken systems, politics, prisons, crimes, felonies
A shutdown shuts us up and then shuts us down
Corruption now normal, once hidden underground
Children abused, misused, or even missing out of sight
An empty swing set, squeaks and sways silent in the night
What is our birthright, what do we all deserve
Leveraging leaders forget the masses they are supposed to serve
The power of the people must stand up and have its say
And so I pause … and so I pray

Moving from the outward to the inward in one brief motion
I see where I must first put my energy and devotion
Delusions – a free-for-all for the sickened mind – hold no power
As we evolve … in the end … in the final hour
We hold out for the truth, and we envision the best
The illusions dissolve and die, and are simply laid to rest
I've got to get out of my head, out of my own way
And so I do what I must do, even in this passion play
In contemplation and meditation, the chaos and static simply fades away
Because I pause … and because I pray

If I Start to Cry, I Will Never Stop

There is a well of grief that, if tapped, could release a spring of tears that may appear endless. Even so, I do believe at the end of the pain and the end of the tears is where eternity begins.

When I recall the moments when my life's dreams were dashed
When I start to stall on momentum that has slowed down so fast
When I see the crashing of monuments that meant so much to me
When I see that the crabs in the bucket want no one to be free
When I think of all the secret and subtle times my mom and dad tried
I wonder how long it would last … if I laid down and cried
I find myself isolated, lost, deserted, corrupted, caught
Believing … if I start to cry, I will never stop

When I picture a boy shut up in a lonely room
Looking towards the ceiling, only imagining his doom
When I look back and see how invisible I was, not standing up for myself
When I think of all the times I put my needs, wants, visions on a shelf
When I perceive how silly miscommunication could push us
off the path of love
When I get a glimpse of the divine mosaic printing perfect patterns,
all seen from above
All the enemies we branded, demanded, attacked, battled, fought
As I now wonder … if I start to cry, will I ever stop?

The family and friends I so desperately longed to know
Can be found beyond the barrier of this facade sideshow
In surreal moment, I once mourned so deeply the death of the living Christ
Not yet knowing that no such darkness can ever extinguish the Light
On Rumi's divine field we shall gather, and meet all the
grand characters there
Into eyes we will recognize, the cast on Shakespeare's stage … now bare

Enveloped in the shimmering illumination that this cycle of birth
and rebirth has taught
Now believing ... as tears wash me clean, this love will never stop

WHEN I LOOK INTO MY HEART

*One morning, I woke up to a hurting heart. I decided to simply write a poem
from the open-minded vantage point of what I see when I look within.
I was surprised to see what I found.*

When I look into my heart of hearts
I find what tears this world apart
A world of war and battle and disease and strife
A world of hatred and anger over this unfair life
A world of gangs and tagging and bravado and stances
A world of dirty tricks, drive-by shootings and angry glances
A world of deep longing and loss and desperation
A world of grief and fear – a world of separation
Where does it all begin; how did it ever start?
I find the answer in my heart of hearts

It's Isabel and Louise who turned away without a word
Leaving me lost, confused, alone – so hurt
It's Kelle with her innocent yet mischievous grin
Before her alcohol, drugs and past did her in
It's a father and a mother who wanted no signs of feeling
Nothing of what I had to say would hold any meaning
It's a best friend Jamie moving far away – a defector
It's a sister – my enemy – though I was supposed to protect her
It's a kindergarten room, like a prison with a guard
It's the bully who made walking to school just so hard
It's a teacher who graded me – F, S or E
Even my own art I could no longer see
My identity was put so far up onto a shelf
I lost it all; I lost myself

When I look into my heart of hearts
I find what tears this world apart

My perception, my vision, my filter, my take
Leaving behind myself – my first mistake
It took my writing, my prose, my creativity
It stole my confidence and imagination and ingenuity
It took my enthusiasm, my joy, my innocence
In the depths, it took everything that made any sort of sense
Leaving only the news of the day, with all its dismay
And the heartbreak and anxiety, sure signs of decay
Though when I peer deeper than this surface show
The reality still resides – the beauty forever exists below
I restore, reclaim, remember what has always been
I find the self – and the truth – I am that I am that I am
I find the chance to begin again, with a brand new start
When I look into my heart of hearts
When I look into my heart of hearts

APOLOGIES FROM A MADMAN

I have this rage that comes flying up at times. It's not good, especially for those within earshot who really don't need that aggravation in their space. And so yes, I do have regrets.

From inside the cage, I display
Red
No other thoughts exist in this state
Of despair
As if I didn't care
But alas I do
That is at issue
Banging the bars – clank, clank, clank
Years ago, my head and heart sank
Walking alone, walking away, walking the plank
To my demise
No surprise
I'm left alive, but stuck in this pain
Stuck in this empty can
In ruins, there is only one thing that remains:
Apologies from a madman

I am sorry for times that I got loud
Distanced from the observing crowd
Wandering lonely as a cloud
My shroud covers over a face gone dark
Stark
The only remarks are those with poison tip
Aimed aimlessness at invisible targets
On walls and ceilings – that hold me in
Pinned
Echoes of hopes and dreams that are dimmed

I shake my head and heart as hard as I can
Giving into the one last ditch effort plan:
Apologies from a madman

Mad at the prison I created out of limiting beliefs from the past
Mad at the concrete and blinding thoughts with fire firmly cast
Mad at the shadows that whispered lies into my ear
Mad at the lovers who once thought of me lovingly and dear
Mad at the broken dreams that shattered when I fell to fear
Mad at the betrayals from friends who left me all alone
Mad at the family who let me hurt, isolated, in our family home
Mad at the illusions I built believing I could not be me
Mad at the closing of my eyes, that once could clearly see

And then silence
Silence
Silence
And sorrow
Looking for a rising Sun birthed in tomorrow
As I borrow another stolen, undeserved opportunity
To make it right
To bring in the light
An illumination that was there all along
Through every one of my out-of-tune songs
Transforming the wrongs
Within me and in within everything that I see
Let me arise to be who I can be as a man
Let me stand tall now, when in the past I ran
A steady rock replaces the shifting, slippery sand
Let me do everything, everything, everything I can
Let me offer ... apologies from a madman

A Prayer for the Burdened

Yes, as we move along our life's path, sometimes it just seems freaking hopeless.
Look what we appear to be up against. If burdened, then let us go within.

Crumbling under weight
I carry for no reason
My shoulders and back burdened
By life
By the invisible band of thieves, muggers and murderers
By the streaking tear
By the shrieking fear
That tells me lies construed to disguise
All truth to the contrary

My back and shoulders burdened
I collapse into dust, like a tower of controlled demolition
Isolation is my company
No dream left to dream
No inhale, no exhale
The stillness of smoldering embers
In the aftermath of this war against my sanity
Thoughts spiral downward in beliefs all too familiar

It is too late
You are not enough
This is your fate
There is no love

And yet …

As the embers cool
A reminder to the fool
The ash and dust replaced
By the face behind the face

By the Sun behind the eclipse
By the seed buried deep in soil
We play the foil to our foreign, over-dramatic selves
Once burdened – our back and shoulders
Someone has moved aside the boulders
Escaping the cave of eternal death
Plato ushers us around the corner to perceive
All that is truly to be seen
The truth

It is never too late
For a view from above
You control your own fate
You are the love

The Observed Life

We may falter and we may fall. The darkness may have its say along the way. However, there is always hope and another day. (Sheesh, this was not meant to rhyme, but I can't help it by now.)

All we must do is stay present, stay attentive, stay open and be ready to take action when inspired.

A key is to stay alert to what can be called "the observed life."

As Socrates said, "The unobserved life isn't worth living." So, we make sure, in this chapter, to make this life worthwhile. It will be necessary on our journey back home.

BEAR WITNESS

A friend Wendy mentioned how much she has seen in this lifetime, commenting with the phrase how she had to "bear witness" to so much. I said, "Hey, that sounds like the seed of a poem." To embrace a life, we must observe a life. And, over time, there sure is a lot of it. And this can include a couple of amazing pets such as my wife's Hennessy and Wendy's Jonah.

In my time, in this world
I have seen, I have heard
Wondrous highs, tumultuous lows
Unconditional love that only heaven knows
Then harsh and heinous, the gnashing hell
The broken dreams from a wishing well
The full spectrum rainbow, I would know all of this
In my life, I would bear witness

I bear witness
To the F grade red, tests full of error
To the towers collapse after explosions of terror
To bodies piled high in devastated lands
To drone strike murder, no blood on hidden hands
To a president's assassination, the motorcade in Dallas
To the lion trophy catch – killing senseless and callous
To the social media frenzy, virtual arsenals of attack
To the driving accident, there writhed Lucy our dear cat

I bear witness
To past due envelops arriving in the mail
To the aging mirror in distressing detail
To gray around temples and wrinkles around eyes
To false witness that maintains the facade and disguise
To the defeat of my football team, the sea of hands
To the collective sighs of all disheartened fans

To the hungry and cold who live outside on the street
To the children who are sold to the men they must meet
To the death of loved ones, full of grieving and crying
To the hospice where I left my mom; she was dying

Why do we do it? What can this be for?
What could exist on the other side of the door?
Who would be there, would they see all of this?
When all is said and done, I would bear witness

I bear witness
To the majestic wonder of nature's sweet beauty
To the newborn of a mother, the cherub little cutie
To gorgeous artwork born from artisan hands
To the melody and harmony of great rock-n-roll bands
To the garden of flowers, the lavish of green
To the Stanley Cup raised by a king of a team
To the cards and prose from lover to lover
To the spiritual path we all can discover

I bear witness
To sunrises and sunsets, we'll call it a day
To footprints on beach sand as we walk on our way
To birthday cake candles blown out with much joy
To the fun antics of the children, the girls and the boys
To the thrills of the roller coaster at the amusement park
To graduations and weddings – each one a new start
To the big winning flashing lights at a Viejas or a Barona
To the unswerving love of a Hennessy and a Jonah

In my time, in this world
I have seen, I have heard
Wondrous highs, tumultuous lows
Unconditional love that only heaven knows
Truly, none of these I would ever want to miss
For in my life, I would bear witness
I would bear witness

The Heart of a Writer

A writer tends to write about the writer's experience, no matter the highs and lows, or perhaps because of them. I think the inspiration comes from a life worth observing.

my heart
broken
my heart
stolen
taken by gremlins that reside in the underbelly of society's hunger
a hunger that demands money
more and more of it
derailing me from my direction inward and skyward
my heart – the heart of a writer
knowing nothing about spreadsheets, balance sheets, financial strategy,
business plans
taxed – in various ways
taxed, taken, stolen, pulled upon, pummeled, trounced, drowned
wanting only enough oxygen to be able to surrender into the soft down
pillow of the creative
not resting there, not relaxing there – just being
pure
without the pull and push
without the past that delivers another hit
taking one hit after the other, like the chin of a boxer who knows not defense
my heart
my hurting heart
pure beneath, longing within, striving to cry, voice, sing
a song grasped from that which originates inward and skyward
from my heart
free
open
the heart of a writer

A Quiet Night

Had this title for a month after my wife uttered the phrase, "I just want a quiet night." How many of us simply want some peace of mind in a world apparently gone crazy?

As static buzzes in and around my head
Tossing and turning and tossing in bed
As heartache howls to the faraway Moon
Harmonies crash in songs out of tune
As sunburns crack sores openly bared
Feet trapped in quicksand, minds racing scared
I long for the key to unlock bondage chains
I long for soothing touch to alleviate the pains
I long for open doors that lead to expanse
I long for the eloquence of the effortless dance
I long for transcendence, flying high above the fight
I long for the peace of a quiet night

I long for the peace of a quiet night
The plateau of wonder beyond wrong and right
The illuminated sparkle linking people together
Originating from the faraway forever
The open field where we all can gather there
Cradling, like baby girl, gently brushing her hair
The silence shimmering in everlasting light
At home in the haven of the quiet night
In the knowing that battles and wars will be waged
And the bitter will fulfill their destiny rage
And players will act out selfish on the world's stage
On and on, over and over, every single age
In the knowing that limelight lovers will present a two-face
And the news will drool over scenarios, worst-case

I can remain here, near and dear, longing for the truth
Never really needing any broadcast-blast outer proof
I can long for sunsets and sunrises that remind this soul
I can long for fractured parts to become complete and whole
I can long for the vistas that reveal the most glorious sight
And embrace, at the depth, the peace of a quiet night
A quiet night

BENEATH IT ALL

One of those pieces where a perception traverses deep enough to uncover the beautiful unknown.

Raging
Blaming
Shaming
Fingers pointing everywhere – past, present, future
A retreat from peace
Into shadows of regret, reeds grow high blocking the sun
Where is the one?
A silence is devoured by earthquakes that shatter glasses tumbling from
cabinets
My rage
Turning the page
Revealing the frustration beneath it all
Beneath it all
In frustration
The end of anticipation
Into a full-blown cry of bitter consternation
Eyes darting back and forth, to and fro
Where am I to go?
What has begun?
Where is the sanity? Where is the one?
Just a sea of hopelessness and depression beneath it all
Beneath it all

In a closet of darkness – depressed
So much suppressed
A pillow suffocates instead of comforts
Placed squarely upon the mouth
Which longs for breath

As it awaits the death
Shivering and shaking, holding nothing dear
Succumbing to the numbing fright, the paralyzing fear
Beneath it all
Beneath it all

Yet, as acts of terror blind the deepest night
A gentle bird ... somehow ... enters into sight
Crossing the sky on its eternal flight
A glimmering hope brings a shimmering light
Faint at first, like the dawn's first peek
Then exclaiming "free" in a game of hide and seek
We rejoice in the recovery of a truth once known
The third eye has opened; this bird has flown
Now fully illumined we know what has begun
What's passed is passed, what's done is done
And so, awake, we greet the brand new sun
Remembering forever, we are the one
Beneath it all
Beneath it all
Beneath it all

THE GIFT OF YES

Today I saw a photo within one of those Facebook memories.

Not just any photo.

It was one of those photos that stands out, has one take pause. It then offers a message, magically captured within the camera's lens and upon the picture frame.

1000 words? Nay, this would offer, somehow, so many more … at this moment in time, for this mind of mine, anyway.

Here was a daughter and a mother.

On a train.

The young one resting her head upon the shoulder of the mother.

Beyond the veil of a simple train ride – a long, tiring one at that –

I perceived a storyline, the length measured within lifetimes.

For some reason, I imagined that once upon a time these two souls – presently named "Dawn" and "Samantha" – gave each other the gift of a "yes." At some point, in between what we understand as a life on earth, the two spirits looked upon another and decided they would follow through on playing the role of mother and daughter.

As if, the words would have been: "Shall we be born into form once more? Shall we be family? Shall you be mine, and I be yours?"

As if, the answer would have been "yes."
Is such a conversation real? Is there a reality of "another side" and the return here again and again?
Who knows?
Who knows what takes place beyond this mere measly lower plane of awareness?
What I do know, though, is that on some level we all answer the question of whether to relate with another person with a "yes" … or "no." It can take place in the most simple way: a first date, a neighborhood game of basketball, a support group meetup, a lifetime of marriage.
It reminds me of the Joni Mitchell song "Secret Place." It goes like this:

> *Out of all of the girls that you see*
> *In bleachers and cafe windows*
> *Sitting flirting with someone*
> *Looking to have some fun*
> *Why did you pick me?*
> *For the secret place*

Think of all the relations that have taken place – for a season, for a lifetime, for a reason – wherein on some very real level, both of you decided to join here in experience.
On whatever level the choice was made, for better or worse, for the sake of lessons and growth, for the grand life experience that relationships can bring … once upon a time we made an agreement.
This is the story that this photo told me today. It's a sweet one … full of mystery, purpose, and beauty.
We are indeed blessed.
Whenever we recognize the gift that is "yes."

THE BATTLE OVER YOUR MIND

Along our journey, it's important we hold onto the sane part of our minds. With all the TV programming, media propaganda and government narratives, it's important we keep our heads on straight.

There is a battle you may not see
A battle for silent slavery
One opened and one closed door
The great Armageddon tug of war
The pull of hatred, the pull of love
To determine finally what you're made of

They want you; they need you
To question everything that you do
To turn from inner guidance proof
To buy the vile and distorted truth
To side with dark shadows of fright and fear
Hoping your hope will disappear
Cut into brown, red, white and black
Painting a future, preparing for attack
There is a battle you may not see
Cashing in on your slavery

Media mayhem makes you nuts
Mental bruises, bleeding and cuts
Lost are the sacred and the sanctity
You scream in your search for sanity
News forecasts are drizzly and dreary
You collapse in a crush, down and weary
There is a battle for your mind
They need you deaf, dumb and blind

But even in darkest night of the soul
There is something they cannot control
You have your choice; you have your will
That lingering voice … small and still
It never left; it was there at the start
The very first breath, the first beat of your heart
When children ran on simple playground
The smiles and giggles on merry go round
Before grades, punishment and lessons in hate
Before we found reason to hesitate
Learned over time, the dissonant note
Off rhythm and rhyme, a small hole in this boat
Though deep inside we know what is real
It goes against what they've taught us to feel

So, we do away with "they" – we take us back
And return to them the limited view of lack
For, joined are brown, white, red and black
We end the tug of war and endless attack
We're left with a lingering ally and friend
One who never has to retreat or defend
It's all right here, in me and you
We need not question what we do
We need not wonder who we are
The inner message now not too far
We can curtail this mind control today
The media blasts no longer hold sway
We can escape the invisible slavery
While bypassing the battle we can now finally see…

ANOTHER TRAIN

*A pal of mine talked about the resiliency in dealing with the harsh experiences
that come along in life, how he got through one tough gap of life only to turn
around and experience another tough go. It's what he called "another train."
Of course, there will be all types of trains coming down the tracks; we just have
to be open to jumping on or not.*

Rolling, rolling down the tracks
It will return again; it's coming back
Horns blow through intersections; passersby they watch
Unaware how the blindsided can easily get caught
Representing our blindness, our unconsciousness, our pain
There will always be another wreck, always another train

Just when we thought we were in the clear
Another train comes along to strike what's dear
We're hurt by another accident, a smash into each other
Between friends, lovers, partners, sisters and brothers
Another vehicle for the subtle and covert attack
Like a train – burning, churning, blasting – coming down the track

But can this be seen another way?
Not a collision, conflict, accident, delay
But rather a chance to connect if we don't fight it
An opportunity to take the wrong and right it
Can we turn around and see the situation anew?
So we lay down our arms and see what handshakes can do
Can we return to the scene of the crime and the crash?
And remove the flags flying at half-staff
Can we not get struck, but instead jump on at the next stop?
Can we not be blindsided; can we not get caught?
Can we heal the wounds, and remove the weight of the pain?
Since … there will always be another experience, always another train
Always another train

I Think I Need a Nap

*This one may come off a bit silly, but who can't relate to wanting to rest their
weary bones along the path of life.*

I'm running and gunning and raring to go
There's only one speed … and it ain't slow
I'm a kid on the run, all about play
I'm gonna have fun, don't get in my way
But – oh no – what this? Things getting kinda icky
My head is all heavy; my stomach sorta sicky
I'm running out of gas, I'm starting to fuss
I kicked a kid in class, and then later on the bus
My mom says she's just about ready to slap
She finally says, "I think you need a nap"

But now as a teen, I'm mean and I'm lean
No need to rest, just my needs to be seen
I'll hit all the media late into the night
When I'm low on entitlement, I'll just start a fight
I burn the midnight oil, doing schoolwork and studies
Until something or someone shows up – hey, who's your buddy?
Party hearty – my teacher, on my shoulder, she'll tap
She has to interrupt: "I think you need a nap"

Growing and slowing – at some point – oh snap!
I need a, I need a, I need a, I need a …

And so, here I go, to a brand new show
My butt in a lazy boy, energy low
Agitated and gruff, I bark at my wife
It's all too much, what happened to my life?
Oh to be in bed … to sleep it all off
The ache in the head, the sneeze and the cough

I whine and complain, what do I really need?
Could I be insane, this turnip will never bleed
I'll just cuddle alone on this chair, like a cat
And finally, finally declare … "I think I need a nap"

THE APE ISN'T DONE

We all have work to do! A friend of mine in my men's group spoke of our evolution as a male species and used this phrase. There was no way this wasn't a piece of poetry having fun with the concept.

If we did come from apes, and I'm not sure that we did
What if we had stopped, or kept potential hid?
What if we just said, "OK, this banana is enough"
And just quit on evolution, and all that Darwin stuff
Now I like bananas, that is not the point I make
It's much bigger of a context, a broader and deeper take
As ancient as the planets, prior to the birth of stars and suns
Questions arose in mind, just when time and space had begun
Could we all be progressing – originating from an almighty one?
It just that I don't think this ape is really done

Now apes still exist in nature and a few of the zoo's big cages
And mankind may have evolved through the multitude of ages
And if this is all true, what a marvel it all would be
To observe all the progress from the ocean and the tree
Whether born from apes or not, we have truly come a long way
Learning to carve with knives, and ride rafts upon the bay
Then cooking with fire, steam, gas, and then the mighty microwave
And learning to hunt endangered animals we have to try and save
Experiments, inventions, advancements, discovery – everything we have found
This carousel of progress we've been riding – round and round and round
All along the way, we created distractions for amusement and for fun
So much so we'd have to say, the ape ... he isn't done

The wheel and the deal and flying machines
Skyscrapers, newspapers and submarines
Ironing boards, washer-dryers and featherweight vacuums
High-powered showerheads, porta potty bathrooms

Sidewinders, steamships and catamarans
Knotts, Sea Worlds and Disneylands
YouTube, HBO, Netflix, giant TV screens
Meatless beef tips, veggie dogs, vegan ice cream
Electricity, radios, the LED light bulb
Ticketmaster, TickPick, SeatGeek, StubHub
Plays, sitcoms, shorts and feature movies
Quantum physics, string theory, newly discovered galaxies
IPads, iPods, iEverything, iPhones
Smores and scones and beef-filled dog bones
Pacman, Tetris, Minecraft, new video games
Bombs, facemasks, Molotov cocktail flames

Now after all this effort, time and space, is this where we are at?
Or is it just an illusion, some more propaganda bullcrap
In either case, why would it stop, why would this be the end all?
Can you imagine if the ape said that before Darwin came to call?
No, it's time to know, there ain't no curtain or a conclusion of the show
We all have so much more learning to do, and so much further to go
So put your banana down for now, pick up a new thought instead
Perhaps the next evolution doesn't belong in the sea, tree or head
Perhaps we complete a circle's journey, and return to the almighty one
Either way, no matter what, it must be true … this ape is just not done

THE BIGGER PERSON

This one is dedicated to all of us wanting a chance to express ourselves in the most expanded way, finding ourselves in an expansive field where we all belong.

In a world separated by the soulless
In a nation scattered in the dark
In a society tattered by the hopeless
In a home shattered into parts
Who will be the bigger person?
Beyond the path of wrongs and rights
In sweet surrender this one will listen
No need for victory in all these fights
Who will be the bigger one?
Expanding beyond the great divide
Who will take a walk in the sun?
With the entire humanity alongside
Who will give space for healthy debate?
Where opposing voices have their say
Who will put behind them the heat and hate
With room for trails on broad pathway
When will all the walls come down?
When will minds and bodies find rest?
When will stands be taken on common ground?
When will we all pass this trickster's test?
No, not to acquiesce or cower or shrink
Not to cave, quit, give up, or give in
But to meet on fields where we consider, ponder, think
And then seek to understand … and listen
Who will be that magnanimous soul
As masks and swords are placed to the side
Who won't rest until we are complete and whole
And there are no barriers behind which to hide?

Who will yield to another but be protected still
No longer slave to righteousness and fear
Holding space for a collective freewill
Where needs are met with every bended ear
Who among us all will be the first
When all is said … and all is done
Quenching everyone's hunger and thirst
Who will be the bigger one?
Who will it be, angels hear a sacred call
Relations ever bonding – never to loosen or worsen
The deeper connection, come one and come all
Who will it be … the bigger person

THE SAME MAN

As we move along our chosen pathway, we may just be shown to be a single actor, wearing various costumes and masks. Not such a bad thing, given how many lessons we must grasp and learn along the way.

Prisoner, guard, convict, thief
I am all and none of these
Burglar, speedster, judge, police
Playing the game of hide and seek
Embracing all, in one big breath
Give me liberty or give me death
Parts to be acted in God's odd action plan
I am … the same man

I am the one who just stole your car
The one who stumbles out of that seedy bar
The gambler who lost it all in a risky bet
Then presses a gun barrel right against my neck
The mugger whispering in ear: "your money or your life"
The cheater who cheated with your dear, sweet wife
The liar who lies … into eyes … all of the while
The realtor, banker and lawyer who smiles that slippery smile
The addict that scrounges aimlessly for the next high
The numbed-out who doesn't even know how to get by
I am the monster, the rapist, the beast, the foe
With nowhere to be and nowhere to go
The solider, armed and dangerous, ready to attack
The enemy, armed and dangerous, prepared to fight back
The rich tyrant dictator with the most evil of plan
The beggar on street corner with outstretched hand
I am … the same man

The hero, the wizard, the saint, the sage
The next messiah bringing forth a brand new age
The eagle that soars to heights of the highest perch
The freedom-seeker who frees all who will search
The one who walks the elder from one curb to the other
I am the love of the uncle, the son, the father, the brother
I am the medicine man who cares for all in this tribe
I am the sharing friend with nothing to hide
I am the supportive ear when you have lost so much in life
I am the steady strength guiding you back into the light
I am the guardian protecting you from the threatening force
I am the provider representing life's abundant source
The partner who knows what's mine … is mine to share
The lover who caresses in kindness and care
The magician whose curiosity invites all to understand
The warrior who plants the stake and then takes a stand
The king who carries in heart the most inclusive of plan
I am … the same man

And in my own mundane life ... I too play the parts
Breaking and blessing and rescuing hearts
As pressures and stressors continue to mount
As avalanches collapse upon each bank account
I hold steady to the truth an identity strong
As in "The Who's Down in Whoville" celebration song
No force can turn me from the right to the wrong
No one can seduce me away from where I belong
I'll stand in presence – through failure and success
Doing what I must, and doing my best
I'll falter at times, and I'll break down in defeat
And yet brush myself off and get back on my feet
No matter where I go or who I have become
Nothing in my past will have to be undone
Moving forward into storm, breaking through the storm cloud
Taking flight into sunlight, with a voice bellowing loud

I am here – for you and me – in God's destiny command
I ask that – through it all – you come to understand
I will always be … the same man

SANTA IS REAL

*Newsflash – everything you thought before just may be false …
especially if it was negative.*

OK folks, here what's true
Uh-huh, so here is the deal
Turns out … who the hell knew?
Yes … Santa is real!
Now I know what you're thinking
You may be thinking that I'm nuts
But I've got a suspicious inkling
There's no ifs, ands or buts
It came to me while walking
It came to me today
My wife and I were talking
And I just had to speak up and say
Hey, Santa is real, it turns out!
This was the epiphany
On top of roofs, we should shout
Someone alert a symphony
Music and bells should blast
Children shall be alerted
An eternal Saint Nick at last
No longer are we deserted

Now this may all appear too deep
Or what's the word: "esoteric"
It may all exist behind sleep
Transcending all that's barbaric
It's abstruse, obscure, arcane
Enigmatic, inscrutable or abstract
Cryptic, complex, complicated … insane
Or simply devoid of fact

But maybe it is profound
What I learned on my walk today
Heck, it's simply what I've found
As I try to find my way …

If we can make up war
And devils of every kind
From the excitable to the bore
We create everything we find
If we can make up the daily news
Whether real or imagined true
Singing to glory or the blues
Knowing what we always knew
If we create our own reality
We choose what we must defend
Selecting the senseless or the sanity
Defining our enemy and friend
They say Adam named everything
Everything he put his hand on
And now we've learned how to sing
As the band steadily marches on
If the eastern spiritual dudes
Can determine all is an illusion
We are making up all our feuds
And embracing the dull delusion
Now lovers fight over nothing
Angry, they both try to act so tough
Looking for substance in the something
We make up all this stuff
Into a hurricane we can be hurled
Searching for eternal love
And stumble along in a secret world
With Gabriel's "What was it we were thinking of?"

So, if we can be so inventive
And manifest a world like this
Can we find a deeper incentive?
And follow our own true bliss
Can we imagine a world in kind
And picture ourselves in a boat on a river
What is it we could ultimately find?
Where could we be finally delivered?

In a world of pure imagination
We could even eat all the dishes
Overcoming all consternation
Diving into the well of wishes
Here is where we can start anew
The depth of what we see, know and feel
Where acceptance, love and giving … is true
And – yes – Santa is real
Yes … Santa is real

YOU WERE NEVER ALONE

There are many forms of addictions: those behaviors and strategies designed to protect us from the loss, loneliness, and pain. After some time, through the love and grace of God, no longer does the addiction support an avoidance that could never last. You would always have to come to the end of a road where even an addiction could not protect you. Thank goodness.

When the escape hatch busts and will not work
When distractions become emotional reactions
When there are no more pain blockers for all of the hurt
When the avoidance and drugs no longer take traction
Addiction becomes restriction with all its friction
There is a brick wall at the end of that road
The darkness smirks as it achieves its dark mission
All that sparkling glitter – now only false gold
You're left with your lonely self and the wounds of the past
And the reasons you started using and abusing at the start
And all of the excuses that would never really last
You're left with an abandoned, overlooked, broken heart

So what do you do then when nothing else will work?
Beyond the band-aids covering an invisible scar
The elusive longing, the hidden hands, the buried hurt
Release, freedom, happiness – they're seen from afar
Alone, alone, alone – how did I get so far off track?
Where can I go and what can I do?
Home, home, home – how can I get back?
A whisper tells me what I already knew
We choose to move on, move away ... and face inward
To destinations that have at least half a chance
With a nod to the angels, we look skyward
And breathe, sing, pray, breathe some more ... dance

Fear brought you here, but it is here that you will be freed
A broken heart still carries all the heart that you could hold
From the moment you were born, it was all agreed
The greatest story that will ever be told
You are offered everything that you could need
You aren't truly left out of the garden divine
Your soul embraces the sacred seed
And all that you needed to leave behind
Healing, in the end, starts with the removal of all delusion
The false prophets, puppets and idols – it will be shown
The release of addictions and escape hatches will be a solution
As well as the knowing … you were never alone

THE UNEXPECTED GUEST

Inspired only by the words "unexpected guest" in an e-mail from a friend. I knew there was a poem in there, not knowing about the Agatha Christie play of the same name. I decided to write this poem with just the title in mind, not knowing who would be behind these doors in my mind. I was surprised to see who showed up.

Cloaked with robe
A mysterious messenger
Arises
In doorway
Holding the key
Of the great mystery
To all the universal gifts, eroding the rifts
Bringing balance, reflection, harmony, all of our best
Who is this unexpected guest?

Entering the door
Who is this one here for?
Taking a seat, the suspense grows
Removing the hood
All is understood
As if in dreamscape
As if by miracle
By fate
Beyond the realm that carries enmity, anger, hate

Beyond separation
Here in full unification
The end of anticipation
The presence, our visitor
Alone
But joined in history's thread
To those I would love, honor, fear and dread

With repeated removal of garment mask
Revealed at last …
Revealed at last …

My first friend
Who ran and jumped in puddles
Along with me
Wild abandon, wicked, mischievous and free
Reminding me of everything I need to be

My first schoolteacher
Who gave me smiley faces and knew me well
Somehow
Wanting the best for me
To go beyond the "S," and earn that "E"

My first fight
The bully who would try and get me in headlocks
Steal my Pop Tart
My milk money
Until a crazed monster flew out of me
And stood my ground
For my safety … safe and sound

My first girlfriend
Who recognized something in me, anyway
A heart beating
A feeling fleeting
Before time and tears washed it all away

My first heartbreak
Sitting still, staring off, glazed eyes
Wanting this not to be real
The cracking Earth, the letter, the goodbyes
Echoed in the memory of each love torn apart
An education in the will of the wind … and the will of the heart

My father
Buying Slurpees
Playing catch
Watching ballgames
Attending graduations, celebrations, presentations
Without a word
That ellipses within communication …
A timetable of subtle and silent support

My mother
Looking back to her the first day of kindergarten
Making sure she is there
And will remain
Ever present, ever loving, ever strong
For all time
Even after the pain
And the hospice … and the final kiss
Upon forehead

My wife
Standing side by side
We ride the wildest ride
Learning of connection without compromise
The holy instant grasped in fingertips
The haven that is a holy relationship

My life
Who I need to be
Striving for the excellence of a report card "E"
With a heart known no matter what
Surviving the deepest of the deepest first cut
In silent support found within
A look back in memory where it all could begin
The holiest of holies – we stand face to face
In the presence of the people I have come to embrace

Every character in this play
Made me who I am today
With or without iambic meter
The rose could not be any more sweeter
Every one of these revealing something of myself
Something to take down, in time, from high upon a shelf
As I place everyone and everything, finally to rest
Revealed at last …
The unexpected guest

WITHOUT GUILT OR DEFENSE

You know what they say: if you act defensive, you are normally hiding some form of guilt or regret. Now a world without either? Hmmm, that would be heaven.

Imagine a world without guilt or defense
No need to be spurred on into attack or offense

No need to hide behind masks of misdirection
Transparency would dismiss all need for inspection
The open cage would cease all corporal correction
Leaving spirits free to realize the one true resurrection

With such freedom, we would reveal all that junk, all that stuff
Without fear, we could reveal the "I'm not good enough"
No thoughts "I am less than" "I am more than" and "I am bad"
No leverage for the vicious victor who gloats "I am glad"

No rather …

A coy glimpse under cloak to unveil a shining light
A cord of connection – the string to the soaring kite
A fulfilled promise of an innocent and eternal life
The curious mind, which would listen – in wonder – as a friend spoke his word
The attentive ear that would comfort all who just want to be heard
The unarmed human, defenseless, in a now safe and sane world

Imagine a world…

THE TURNING POINT

Ah, my favorite part of the journey, this is the "turning point." Here is where the change begins. After the initial start of the expedition, following the meeting with the challenges and monsters along the path, and beyond the observation necessary to make educated decisions, there comes that moment.

It is the point of transformation – where the spiraling downward becomes the shift upwards, where the tanker begins its U-turn, where the direction is suddenly homeward bound. We have traversed far enough away from our home, and now it's time to turn back, towards our rightful place. We can follow the breadcrumbs back to where we once began, but with a sack full of experience and life lessons.

Here we come …

What Can I Do?

Facing so much adversity in our lives – notably in the political arena where politicians rule – I ask myself: do we have the power to make a change, have we lost the power, or is it something we can always reclaim if we wish? These are the thoughts that led to this poem.

Politicians smile, all the while, making up their own mandates
People with ballots are left with a total of two candidates
At the end of the day, laws are passed without our say
At any time, the DUI stop can stand as a delay in our way
We're chastised with "Ignorance of the law is no excuse"
In courtrooms we question if we can push back and rebuke
If we've been conditioned to just follow orders and toe the line
No wonder it feels like we're trying to come back from behind
Trying to climb our way out of the burdened debtors' prison
Credit card companies alter agreements – their own decision
The bosses decide your worth with their almighty power
Bathroom breaks are available on every fifth half hour
The stealing of our sovereignty – who did this? Who?
Like dead body floating to the surface: "Eh, what can you do?"

What can you do when the Congress celebrities rule the net
And media pundits spout out their opinions on the boob tube TV set
We sit back, as passive public, hoping we can get our needs met
Having to focus on our lives, and an American Dream to get
Meanwhile bigwigs get by untethered, unnoticed, untaxed
And the media slides by playing up their own clumsy facts
And the corrupt leaders glide by without preserving what's true
Like someone missing the bus, shoulders shrug – "Eh, what can you do?"

A great question we can ask ourselves, as countrywomen and men
Harking back to the beginning, to see how this could end
No more couch potato surfing channels for a world of pretend
But standing up, and focusing on what we need to preserve and defend

Patriots, with the backbone of a healthy and sturdy constitution
Remembering that initial move towards freedom and revolution
Fighting a good fight, bugle cry falling on ears not deaf
A courageous call for "Give me liberty or give me death"
A call for action, all along, even in slumber ... we knew
We could always serve, in action, asking, "What can I do?"
Let us all ask now – "What can I do? What can I do?"

GET MOVING

When the going gets tough, the tough get moving. What else is there to do?

Get moving
Get grooving
There is no time to waste
You in the hurry and the haste
And your desire to get a roommate
Before it's too, too, too late

Sometimes I hate being on the planet
It's not like I really planned it
With the slow degrading and degradation
I want a celebration and a graduation
To a higher world, a higher place
Show me the face beyond the original face
The one my father's father's father had
Back before kids did things that were good or bad
Life ain't no picnic, nor is it just a party
All joy, all fun, all games ... hardly

Get me out of here, out of this suffering
While my motors race and my computer is buffering
I run and run and run and then I run some more
Just to get to a place where I was before
Before all this stress and these financial fits
Before we had all this crap we thought we had to get
Before we gathered all these possessions that possess us
Forgetting that our true source is the only thing to trust

Get me home, take me now, take me back
So weary from all the thoughts that attack

Get me home, I demand it right now
I'm ready for final curtain call and bow
Say goodbye, fare thee well, and goodnight
Time to turn off and then truly see ... the light

A MILLION SOLUTIONS

It is said that with every problem, a solution arises simultaneously.
Too often we may forget to even look.

We walk around, clueless behind our mask
Lacking direction or deep introspection
Leaving behind inquiry, the questions to ask
Erasing resolutions with swift deflection
An attitude stoic, a reality stark
Dissolving into distrust, the mighty delusions
Roaming blindly, not kindly, into the dark
Not recognizing … a million solutions

Problem mode is our honor code
We align with guru Debbie Downer
Not a unique path, a less-traveled road
We're the lost soul, the out-of-towner
Let's quit before we even start
A victim's hope for reparations, restitution
Placing our horse way behind the cart
Bypassing the answer in a million solutions

A million solutions – showing us the way
A million solutions – surrounding us every day
A million solutions – fueled by love
A million solutions – could they ever be enough

Turning this meandering tanker around
Time to wake up to the truth, as we must
Turning things right-side-up from upside down
Turning the doubtful back towards the trust
Overcoming the obstacle that blocks out the sun
Uncovering our eyes that can now see the light

The end of the ending, the beginning just begun
Discarding the wrongs, and embracing the rights

Home, here we are, we didn't go far
Not when we finally see where we stand
Not a faraway wish, nor a faint distant star
Just the result of entering a promised land
Eyes now wide open, a broken heart healed
Piercing a murky mind's confusions
Pulling our head out, pathways no longer concealed
From the quandaries and quagmires ... a million solutions

A million solutions – in this moment, paving the way
A million solutions – gloriously arriving this very day
A million solutions – fueled purely by the everlasting love
A million solutions – finally, finally, finally enough

DETOX

What do we do with all this junk and gunk that accumulates in life and in our mind? Every one of us has an answer within us, and once we apply the answer, our lives shall turn a corner.

Detox
Sediments of sickness
Ill feelings, grudges, resentment
Caked onto the brain
Weighing down the free flow of thoughts and emotions
Detox
Flushing out toxins
Flushing down the drain
Releasing, exiting, freeing thoughts and emotions
Fear runs into hiding
Sadness wipes tears away
Anger bellows out the cry of the night
Detox
The blockage in arteries
The caked-on gunk and junk
Found in unnatural food
And your intestines and bowels
The damned-up bronchial tubes that long for oxygen flow
The tobacco stench that violates the esophagus
The physical aches and pains that originate
From the original pain found in hidden thoughts and feelings
Gone astray, gone awry
Without the wings of flight
Or the wisdom to detach, denounce, deconstruct
Detox

You're Not Welcome Here

*In the end boundaries must be drawn, cutting away that which does not serve us
or even reflect our truest nature. It can be a beautiful farewell.*

Shyness whispers in my ear; despondency responds
One sure truth is all so clear, nowhere do I belong
As friends disappear, there comes to mind a lonely open door
The past appears, and now I recall the losses from before
There are no real surprises … just the echoes down the hall
And then the belief arises: "You're not welcome here at all"

An absent mother didn't see the medals I could have worn
A jealous brother oh so mean, saying: "It was better before you were born"
Hide and seek in the yard, you all played it without inviting me
Math and speech so hard, I could barely manage a D
There were the cliques in high school, the athletes would gather inside
You know I just wasn't that cool, the elites kept me outside
The dates I had were blah, and the relationships were fine
Yet fate would lead me blind, until connections left me behind
One betrayal after the other, I question if I can go on
Can I handle another chance to see where I don't belong?
Not ever knowing where to start, or when to say what to say
And then even my own heart, found a way to keep me at bay
With little gratitude, I saw only the lack before my eyes
Even in solitude, my thoughts would attack my own disguise
Holding up a tight clenched fist, no relief, just a trip turning into a fall
Arising from a mindset mist, that belief: "You're not welcome here at all"

And then alas it does come: a new mind, a new thought
No matter how far I've run, it was time that I got caught
Gradually, from place to place, the movement had begun
Finally, face-to-face, I saw the reflection of the one

Let's hold it out, give it birth, and breathe a brand new breath
Let's scream and shout, in our rebirth, seizing a timely death
A healed mind realizes what to do, and also what to know
A feeling kind, a path so true, in this time to grow
Full of grace and with loving release, we cut away what does not serve
With a steady pace, we shift beliefs, and accept what we deserve
Could the original thought be wrong, could we halt a belief gone astray?
Could it be that I do belong, in a reality where it's safe to say?
Yes, just in time, we secure a new phase, heeding the angels' call
And now we decline and return the phrase:
sorry ... you are not welcome here at all
You're not welcome here at all

AT LAST

Be aware of those violent voices … especially the ones that arise from within.
These will be transformed over time, ultimately, as we take command
of a direction we wish to proceed.

Shouts of doubt
The avalanche of harsh critique
Mild and meek, we attempt our retreat
Under the crush of it all
Yet our shields cannot protect us
From that which tears at us from within
We cannot win
The devil's double-dare enrolls our participation in our own demise
We fall for the lies
We are not wise
The guillotine of self-loathing leaves us broken, scattered
What matters to a lonely soul without purpose or drive?
We must survive
And so we take up the fight to stay alive … at last
Not silencing or shushing the voices without reason
We embrace the treason
Stationing shouts of doubt no longer at the helm of this ship
But rather under our wing
This lonesome, sweet, little thing
We protect it, not neglect it
We reveal it, not conceal it
We love it, not hate nor berate it
Inner demons hold no power
When engulfed in our mindful presence
A lasting essence
Delivering us to peace, at last, peace

TO THE GHOSTS

This was written in 1994. I remember sitting at a Lakeside diner with a girlfriend, writing this out on a napkin in the days I was deeply into emotional healing work. When you imagine the truth of the light, it's easy to see the illusions that attempt to cover it up.

To the ghosts who tell me the worst
To the shadows who just don't understand
To the monsters who place themselves first
I must say: "Your voice cannot command"

I used to accept you all
As you comforted me in my shell
We'd glorify our graceless fall
In this prison – a lifeless hell

Your voices told of maim
And mayhem as a victim
Perception came from blame
Not from clarity or wisdom

But now I say "No thank you"
You've done all you could and more
For now it is so pure and true
The light is what I'm living for

GATEWAYS TO HEAVEN

I woke up this morning with a thought – "Hey, there are gateways to heaven!"

Just like there are windows to the soul in the eyes of sentient beings, there are gateways or windows to heaven in so many visible and invisible parts of our world.

- ~ A child's giggle
- ~ A pet's wagging tail wanting a walk with you
- ~ A mother's phone call message ... "Just wanting to know you are OK"
- ~ A father's proud, nodding head when you aren't looking
- ~ A brother's mocking poke that simply says he cares enough
  to notice your bad hair day
- ~ A niece's custom-made friendship bracelet
- ~ A girlfriend's or boyfriend's or wife's or husband's support through
  the hard times
- ~ A bird finding the water in the front yard fountain and its magic ways
  to let the rest of the flock know
- ~ A wink and a nod from the serendipity and deja vu experiences
  signifying the Universe's gentle nudge

May we be open to the countless, infinite apertures that let in the light and not fight against the molehill of evidence glorifying the darkness.

May we bow to the gateways, a blessing for eyes ready to see their eternal truth.

DIVING INTO FAITH

Poet David Whyte has a poem that starts "I want to write about faith."
I too wanted to write about it, perhaps borrowing a certain meter.
At the end of the darkness, there really is no other choice but to dive into
this unknowable knowing.

Faith.
I want to dive into faith.
Into the cool, blue water that embraces me like a womb.
Safe.
Assured.
Peaceful, restful.
Originating all from faith.
Faith.
That link to something higher – pure. Like cool, blue water.
Beyond the fear.
Beyond the stress.
Beyond the doubt.
That dreaded doubt that would laugh at my failures, even the most minute
of mishaps, exclaiming, "This is the real you. This is how it will continue.
This has just begun."
Those terror remarks that rattle my sense of self, and implode my inner core,
like strategically placed detonations in old, creaky building.
Blueprints with plans to ruin me at every turn.
If not for…
If not for…
Faith.
The knowing that these shadows are temporary, only existing because some
fiend has blocked the Sun … for a moment.
Faith – the keen and clear awareness that the Sun does assuredly exist behind
all shadows.
The Sun – the source.

The source of heat, warmth, and life.
Creating a glimmering reflection off the cool, blue water.
Forever.
No matter the frightful remarks from a mind bent on destruction.
Forever.
In faith – in life.
In life.
That which exists in every breath into lungs.
Filling and emptying, filling, and emptying.
When observed, taking us infinitely deeper into the truth that will free us.
To love.
To faith.
To faith.

I Want to be Closer to Thee

*This one is about that longing again, on that sacred journey, to return home,
to how it used to be.*

I want to be closer to thee
Lately it's been just me, me, me and me
I want to feel that moment, that link
The one in between the breath, right before the blink
The connections with spirit, the masters and guides
The haven where there are no barriers, no distinctions, no sides
To meet on common ground in the invisible reunion
A visit with archangels, in a safe setting of communion
I want to feel happy, joyous and free
I want to be closer to thee

I want to be closer to thee
To loved ones I have been too busy to see
To friends whose friendship I wish to rekindle and recall
To pals sharing the past, celebrating it all
To foes I have shunned, shamed and judged
With all the bitterness of the grumble and the grudge
I want to set you and myself free
I want to be closer to thee

I want to be closer to thee
The one I am to discover in destiny
The one I truly perceive in the reflection of the mirror
The soul whose image comes in clearer and clearer
The reappearance of a "self," one residing deeply within
Being where I am, embracing where I have been
Imagining the future, but knowing of a presence
The illuminating light, the deepest yet brightest essence
The one pure and prominent identity
I want – so deeply want – to be closer to thee...

INTO HEAVEN'S PROMISE

*With all the noise of the world, there must be something more. I understand there
to be a promise regarding that which resides beneath everything.
I understand it to be heaven.*

Rumbling and tumbling, this heart aches
Constricted, constrained, contorted
How long before the awakening
Before the earthquake that alleviates the pressure
Holding breath, holding back
Imagining pouncing tigers around next corner
I fight the devil futility
What is the cure for this ache, this snake's grip?
Media infiltrates mind and poisons its stream
Then joins forces with predictions of gloom
Some, my own

I wait impatiently for relief
But also act
Actively expressing the tremors that hint at destruction
Actively revealing the faith in invisible watchers
Actively moving towards the light
Within
In active prayer I plead for rebirth
Born anew into a moment of peace
Into heaven's promise, secretly offered like a playful child's whisper
Like a breeze across face at ocean cliff
Like an eyelash kiss of hovering angel
In the warmth of mother's blanket wrapping up to the chin
In the safety of a daddy's back carrying us onward
In the love that lingers behind this all

Sounding siren, we hear the call
Bracing for the end of the mystery and the misery
The end of the charade, the end of the ache
Into the truth, into the heart
Into heaven's promise

INVOLVE HER

An online yoga teacher told her students to continually use the power of the breath during their practice. She made sure to use the phrase "involve her" when referencing that life-affirming breath. How quaint, how poetic.

Restricted, restrained, we hold back the power
We hide, we've lied, we cling and then cower
We hold on, we hold on – waiting for that perfect space
We hold on, we hold on – grasping for something safe
We're blind to the bliss, the grand state of glory
We repeat the lines to some old, worn-out story
What have we forgotten, what don't we consider?
It's the power of the breath – what can we give her?

She is expansion, she is the heights, the breadth
She is the inhale and exhale, she is the breath
The urgency of her sustenance is met when we must
The depth of her being is explored when we trust
The gift she brings originates from a haven high above
The gift of her giving comes from a pure state of love
No longer do we fear her, no longer do we spite her
It is the magnificence of the breath – let us invite her

Nowhere can we go where she does not go along
Nowhere can we flow where the melody misplaces the song
Nothing can invalidate her, nothing can replace her
It is the beauty of the breath – we can only embrace her
The effortless grace found in the interweaving fabric of life
The dark turning to light, before again the day turns into night
The mysterious puzzle, something to behold, we cannot solve her
It is the power and the wonder of the breath – let us involve her
Yes, in the end, as it was in the beginning – let us involve her

THE STILL SMALL VOICE

I went full-on Bruce Springsteen circa 1973 on this one. That was the time the Boss thought he had to rhyme everything. Remember: "Madman, drummers, bummers and Indians in the summer..." I attempted to alter this poem's rhyming scheme a bit, but it wouldn't let me. So here then, another poem with the intention to shift us towards peace.

Shaking in this quake as I lie awake
Everything at stake, yet it all just seems so fake
I try to breathe deep, so I can fall asleep
As beams in the attic creak, and stairways ascend too steep
Cries in the night, howling a burst of terror fright
Pleading for new sight, so that finally I can be all right
Time to be quiet and still, I'm offered an array of new choice
A deeper will, on this day ... a still small voice

A still small voice

Mortgages and bills, join broken dishes and spills
In the freak-out alarmist drills, a dreary prophecy fulfilled
A backache and headache crescendo into heartache
Stop the madness, stop the anger, stop the hate
Boisterous bickering in the head, all sanity has fled
I'd rather hear the music of the spheres instead
Moments to slow down, the subsiding of incessant noise
Reality found, heaven bound, heeding ... a still small voice

The still small voice

Faint like the baby's whisper sigh
The lilting serenity of a mother's lullaby
Recognizing the foibles, the folly and the play
Yet never losing sight of beauty along the way
The still small voice

Nudging gently, in guidance, pointing out a divine plan
Judging not – any race, religion, woman or man
A soft breeze upon the face, always full of grace
Rushing not – but like a stream, moving a steady pace

The still small voice

Now seeing the majesty of the mountains, the clear blue sky
Perceiving the symmetry of the fountains, hummingbird wings as they fly
The mosaic of cause and effect, what we come to know
The horizon ocean line perfect, the colors of the rainbow
The sunset and the sunrise, each time a new surprise
Transcending all man-made lies, as we all arise, arise, arise
Of life, what we make, take it higher, with the one and only choice
After the earthquake a fire ... and after the fire a still small voice

The still small voice

THE GREATEST IMPACT OF ALL

Driving one day, I thought of how much I loved some of those I have lost, and how much this common world seemed so meaningless compared to the truth underneath it all. I pictured the impact that politicians and Hollywood stars have on our lives, and then juxtaposed that against the impact of true friends and family. I just had to laugh.

The ultimate, the highest, the greatest impact of all
It is not found upon this planet, so very small
The building of Atlantis was really no big deal
With everything now underwater, even pillars of steel
Pyramids still stand, yet they bring power in from the sky
Indeed, where is the value from birth until we die?
Where do we point towards a great influence, a grand plan?
Could it even originate from what is built by woman or man?
Arenas for epic competitions hold the theater of the day
We watch on through commercials to see how the grown men play
News and entertainment are fed to us, hungry lizards that we are
Towers fill downtowns, a great wall is visible from the stars
And yet, another invincible skyscraper could surely stumble and fall
What is the ultimate, the highest, the greatest impact of all?

Like the off-key found on an out-of-tune song
A loved one collapses, breaks a hip, and is too soon gone
A loving pooch must be put to rest on the saddest, saddest day
There are no words for such heartache, there is nothing really to say
A void remains where once grace promised it would last
Earthquakes of loss leave buildings and bodies burned – ash to ash
So where is the worth; why do we live; what is the use?
God's mysterious way? God's secret will? Just another damn excuse
But carry on, I guess we shall, I guess we must
Looking for purpose through the trouble and rubble – dust to dust

Those making the rules, control the masses and wield all the power
As politicians rise, the populace divides, reacts, attacks, and cowers
Until the pendulum swings, and the people remember the silent call
Perhaps from the ultimate, the highest, the greatest impact of all

It is born of creation, as below so it is from above
Forever to come from the source that is love
It is born of creation, as below so it is from above
Forever to come from the source that is love

It is love my friend; it is love that ushers in all the meaning
Giving presence and life to every single human being
From a foundation of rock, invisible to the naked eye
To the building of a true home … a haven in the sky
The infinite discovered as we pull on that inner thread
Dipping down into the heart, moving away from the head
Entertained not by actors feigning passion, as in a show
But rather amused by family and friends who we truly know
No sports trophies or academy awards hold any value now
No standing ovation, no curtain call, no curtsy or bow
Just eternal sweet memories that gently float on by
Just the halo aura bright and the glimmer in the eye
In a Garden of Eden after genesis and before the fall
Now we come to embrace the absolute, the greatest impact of all

Born of creation, as below so it is from above
Forever to come from the source that is love
Forever to be seen from spirit's highest view
Where no one and nothing dies, and where everything is new
Where towers are not built on sand, but on the steady, sturdy line
Where powers do not come from man, but from the sacred divine
The true celebration, the force from above
Forever to flow from the source that is love

THERE COMES A TIME

After the turning point, the path is clear — away from delusion and towards a destiny.

There comes a time when all good rhymes
Arrive at the end of the line
When we say goodbye to the lies and disguise
And the façades built to hide
We say farewell and let go
Of the parades and the show
There comes a time
When the roles that we play
Have all had their say
And the costumes that we wear
Out of fear or despair
At last … give way to the sublime
For … there comes a time

There comes a time
When we ascend into the depth
Into that which is left
The ashes left behind
Can only remind
Revealing a truth that stands forever
Crushing status that never could measure
Demolishing everything into dust
Precious metals turn to rust
Melting masks, burning down, ripping free
Unlocking the prison with the key…

Our sweetness, our bliss, our glory
The start to the never-ending story

The light and the love
The raining gifts from above
The purity, the joy
A little girl, a little boy

Finally, in the end
For all family, foes and friends
We'll embrace what is there at the finish line
For always and forever … there comes a time

FINAL REUNION

After a poignant conversation with my wife about our dearly loved pet dog
Hennessy, and the loss experienced there, I had this sense of longing for reunion.
I imagined being able to run towards any lost love again and remain there.
Is there such a reality where we never have to part with any of our loved ones?
Can such a reunion happen at any time, beyond space and time?
These questions led me to this poem.

A farewell song as we all march along
Once a waltz, a dance, a chance to move from me to we
Now walking aimlessly in the street
So incomplete
Kneeling, a heart bleeding for thee
Looking skyward as the rain thumps down
Tears mixing with drain water on the ground
You were here, but now you're gone
A final goodbye as I move along
Alone
Desperate for the memory of union
Searching for … the final reunion

We laughed, we played, we knew the way
We talked about nothing, and it made sense
Jokes made at our own expense
It didn't matter – nothing that we could say
Could ever take away
Or replace
That which we held sacred every day

Only death, the final farewell
The veil, the curtain, hiding heaven and hell
Stripping us of our home in union
Destroying all hope in a final reunion

The final reunion
The last time we have to part
The final reunion
The backtrack to the very start
The final reunion
No more leaving, no more grieving
The final reunion
No doubt remains in our believing

You run back to me as in a dream
It's just like it has always been
A dance, a chance
For love's curtain call … a call for faithful stance
Like a puppy greeting the wayward traveler at the door
I rush eagerly towards the love of my life
I recall what this love and this pain are for
The loss, the longing, the union
The cost, the belonging, the reunion
The sweetest of reunions
One that is, alas, final – the last of its kind
As we reunite in heart, soul, and mind
Finally knowing what was yours and ours … is mine
As everything dissolves in the mist of space and time
In a final rhyme

A farewell song as we all sing along
Now a grand waltz, a dance, a chance to truly see
Now joining in celebration in the streets
Whole and complete
Kneeling, in prayer, a heart open to thee

I WILL START HERE

Inspired by soul-fueled songs like Peter Gabriel's "Solsbury Hill" and John Denver's "Rocky Mountain High," I wanted to write a poem dedicated to my deepest identity beyond personalities and pre-conceived concepts. I struggled with it, but finally finished it after a week. Hope my soul is happy!

Questions pile high, a mountain of confusion
Drenched in mystery, a downpour of delusion
Tailwinds splinter hopes into scattered ships without aim
Until my soul's journey is complete, I will remain
Victimized by mistakes, regrets, guilt, and shame
Tell me please … what is my name?
Whispers of a label belonging to me
Cupped and cradled like a trophy
Ever since chariot guided me towards the Earth plane
With only ripples of a purpose and murmurs of a name
I would start here, commencing again and again and again
With every death, another chapter to close, and one to begin
In the middle of darkness, dodging terror, wonder and fear
I will remain, I will remain … I will start here

With a veil over face, I discover every disgrace
I misplace what it means to be a member of the human race
Ego leads me onwards with pride … and I hide
Unveiling each successive obstacle and barrier … and I collide
Ramming 2 x 4s across my thick skull so that my soul will learn
I collapse to knees once more … looking skyward … I yearn
Yearn for the truth beneath egotistical will
Yearn to overcome the desire to destroy, to overpower, to kill
Yearn to rekindle the heartbeat that has started to sink, slow
Yearn to recall a name given to me so long ago

Before I made a game of herding and corralling cats and mice
Before gathering trinkets and toys, so shiny and nice
Empires with towering monuments, hailing all of my glory
Plaques engraved with platitudes – ahhh – my success story
A wealthy miser, I run and hug the tiny pearl in the shell
A monopoly game to lose, a name to forsake, a soul to sell
Separation, leverage and darkness have come to stake its victory
All the stage is clear, I'm left empty-handed, in the depth of the mystery
Rock bottom, a pauper's tale, what more can I do but disappear?
No … no … I will remain, I will remain … I will start here

So many times around this solar system pathway of a circle
So many races, start to finish, facing hurdle after hurdle
I've been kings, queens, beggars, Robert, Walter, James
I've donned multiple masks, carried countless crosses, taken numerous names
Yet in the end, as it was in the beginning, it starts with just a sound
Realizing there is nothing to have gained,
and knowing there was no one to have found
All that I own, all that I gathered, all that I am … is really His
Without this game, without a name, my soul surrenders to what truly is
In this timeless state, there is no space for the terror or the fear
I will remain, I will remain, I will sustain … I will start here

Unity at This Time

In our society, we have been given so many reasons to divide against each other.
Might there be a reason not to?

We pray for understanding
We want to know why …
… The innocence is tarnished
… And the young ones die
We read the headlines
We see the news of the day
Heartlessness, homelessness
Destruction and decay

We want to believe in something
Something secure and sublime
We long for sanity and sanctity
And unity at this time
Unity at this time

Angry words with loved ones
Fractured pieces, shards of glass
Reflecting shattered memories
Revealing a tragic past
Attacking those before us
The terrorists in our minds
Forgetting peace treaties with family
Forgetting unity at this time

Though, we want to believe in something
Something secure and sublime
We pray for sanity and sanctity
And unity at this time

Yes, it is time – it is time
Holidays and gift-giving make it so
The winter chill brings a hearth of fire
We reach for wisdom we do not know
We embrace the invisible power
We celebrate the intangible force
We overcome the separation of Babel's Tower
We correct that which took us off course
Together, we find our common vision
We discover our common ground
We recover from wounds of division
We empty the box of lost and found
Together we mend the broken pieces
We soothe the aches, the scars, the sores
We surrender fully, as the battle ceases
We find what all of us are looking for

Yes, we want to believe in something
Something secure and sublime
We pray for sanity and sanctity
And unity at this time
Unity at this time

A Return to Beauty

Imagine the wonderous joy of such a reunion. You most likely have experienced it before. Perhaps you met up with an old friend from the past. Perhaps you have traveled to your old home and met up with parents and siblings. Perhaps you've seen the video clips of the soldier returning to a son or daughter, rushing into arms missed for years.

That glorious return. In our storyline here, this is the place of residence after the hero on his or her journey comes back home again.

The circle is complete and so is this lead character. Now back to a state of unity, harmony, and beauty.

Here we are …

THE RETURN OF JASMINE

A piece of prose this time. I had this plush row of jasmine shrubs that decorated one part of my white picket fence, atop the porch, near the number of my home address. Often, I wouldn't even notice whether the shrubs were in bloom or not, but there would be that fragrance. And then after the shrubs died, I would often find myself missing that scent and longing for its return.

I miss the smell of jasmine
Of spring ...
In the times when rain blessed the garden with its magic elixir
More potent somehow than any spell cast by water from hose or tap
In the times when the fragrance arose at the end of front porch
Where the jasmine vines wrapped its arms around white picket fence
Climbing upwards to greet the sky
The marriage of water, plant and Sun giving birth to such a sweet view and such a sweet scent
I so miss the smell of jasmine

The garden, so thirsty now, crying to quench a deep longing
Brown
Starving for sustenance, crying for the care and attention
The memory of beauty and grace peering around defiant branches, leaves and twigs that still hold strong
Throughout the drought
The memory of beauty and grace – alive in minds that recall
Beauty and grace

Memories like those of a child – healthy, hearty and wild
When we'd play hide and seek until the streetlights came on
When freshly cut grass made our arms and legs itch
When falling on pavement guaranteed us red medicine and a band-aid
When the rainy days meant galoshes and games indoors

When eating dinner meant everyone was there
When Momma could play catch on this front lawn
When Momma could walk and talk and remember our names
When Momma was here
Memories
Soft recollections that clench a heart when certain songs play from the
days back then

The smell of jasmine
Some say the roots are still good, the life still present
As the branches wither and dry up – in the scorching rays
And memos decree the death of water schedules
I hold on ... I hold on
To memories – of band-aids, streetlights and catch on the lawn
Of games out front, and smiles and giggles, and a mother's kind voice calling
out ... "Jimmy!"
Like the persevering tree trunk that isn't going anywhere
I will see the drought through
And welcome the sweet scent again
And welcome ... the return of jasmine
The return of jasmine

WHAT COMES AFTER MEDITATION?

For this writing, I did an experiment to see what came through after my morning meditation. Hmmm, the writing only took about 25 minutes. What a nice view!

What comes after meditation?
After some sacred time in contemplation
After the bliss of silent whisper, a surreal song
The gentle reminders of an eternal calm
What arrives after that serene stillness sublime?
Perhaps a few words placed in meter and rhyme
But the one major theme that cannot be denied
Is that there is an outer world, as there is one inside
There is a world not always made of sugar and spice
Upon arising from meditation, there is always this life

Life in all of its many myriads of form
Some I wish to discard; some I wish to adorn
There are parts of life that are, yup, a complete drag
And then the treasures of experiences I'm so glad I've had
There are ups and downs and smiles and frowns
With a circus of every sort of face on the clowns

Yes, this can be a circus with its wacky wacked-out whacks
And stacks of stupidity with attacks from the back
Yet there is also a nature supreme beyond this mere dream
Bringing a beauty, a light, a love – beyond that which is seen
So, what do we with all this after sitting so still?
Surrender to the circus or to God's divine will
Maybe we embrace whatever comes our way
And leave it to the archangels to clear clouds away
Perhaps we bring that inner stillness to all that we have here
Or just carry it closer, as the darkness comes near
Life will bring us everything, in a million different forms
With our inner light, we can weather any turbulent storms
And so, what comes after meditation to this poet's mind?
I imagine some inspiration born of meter and rhyme

TOGETHER THEY ARISE

Rumor has it that life's problems and solutions arise at the same time in this benevolent Universe. That's the rumor anyway. I'm believing it is true.

The problems, the mess
All that I must confess
The communication gone astray, awry
As we watch hopes crumble and the loved ones die
All the silly misunderstandings with words that crash and collide
All the problems that convince us to cower and hide

Not alone do they manifest, not alone do these arise
Calling out for our best, asking us to realize…

The cuts and bruises inflicted upon each relationship
The cutting off of hands extended in companionship
Finding ways to uncover the mayhem, the turmoil and the hurt
Seeing new excuses to find cause to abandon and desert
Pointing out the crap, the issues, the reasons to feel bad
Counting the traps, the tissues, the loss of all we've ever had

Not alone do these manifest, not alone do they arise
Calling out for our best, asking us to realize…

For in the reflection of ever-clear eyes
As we slowly stop the drive to dehumanize
And heed the echoing need to simply harmonize
We gently approach the wicked … with the wise
And yes, the solution and the problem – we realize
Together … they do arise

Our self-hatred is met with a call for self-love
The collapsing fortune asks us what we're made of

The painful past returns when we can face what's coming up
The half-empty can be seen as an overflowing cup
The problems of the other mate is a reflection of our own
The solitary path of the lonely branches off to a village home
The quandaries and the puzzles have a built-in solution
The controlling forces await the corresponding revolution
The mother of invention meets the father of creation
In a union where duality is the one manifestation

Not alone do they manifest, not alone do these arise
Calling out for our best, asking us to realize…
Just as the soaring eagle takes wing and flies
Just as the newborn's peace is heard in gentle sighs
Just as the reflection is pure in the purest of eyes

The fear and the courage …
The pain and the bliss …
The hate and the love …
The problem and the solution … we realize …
Together … they arise
Together … they arise

MEANWHILE THE SUN

This tells the familiar story of observing the surface struggles and yet realizing the deeper truths.

Worry washes over you like a rainstorm without cover
So many slings and arrows – you take yet another
Crimes of the past haunt dark crevices of the mind
When all you needed was gentility – soft, sweet, and kind
Knocking on the head, post-trauma appears to never end
When all you wanted was the voice of a true and trusted friend
We crash hard – if not into fate, then into our own denial
Even though so many other realities arise … meanwhile …

Meanwhile the Sun rises in the east and sets in the west
Meanwhile the Moon signals a time for peace and rest
Meanwhile the Earth keeps spinning, bringing opportunities at every turn
Meanwhile the stars keep shining, an eternity impossible to discern
Meanwhile the perfection of karma, ensures all promises are kept
Meanwhile you carry on … taking the next indicated step

The world is unfair, just like it's intended to be
Forcing us to search for our transcendent destiny
The sojourn can be arduous, the pathway often steep
We pray to our Lord … for our souls to keep
And if we look skyward, we shall never be let down
We pray to our Lord …for our souls to be found
Though bodies and buildings collapse – ash to ash, dust to dust
We climb the stairway before us, taking the actions that we must
So many reasons not to laugh, dance, sing or smile
Even though so many other realities arise … meanwhile …

Meanwhile … Meanwhile …

Not to diminish all of the sorrow and all of the pain
Nor the hits your hummingbird heart must constantly sustain
Yet to recognize and celebrate the existence of another side
One whose perfect presence we need not ever hide
The presence of light, levity, brevity, certainty, and love
The presence of every angelic guide reflecting from above
The presence of our daily bread, taking care of our basic needs
The presence of prayer to the Lord, for our souls to be freed
So much to be seen as bad, wrong, and indifferent … all the while
Even though reasons, infinite, give us cause to pause … meanwhile

Meanwhile the Sun makes its journey, all the way from east to west
Meanwhile the Moon reminds us of our nightly needs to rest
Meanwhile the Earth keeps spinning, round and round evermore
Meanwhile the stars keep shining, urging us towards heaven's door
Meanwhile your beauty, truth and heart can never be denied
Meanwhile you carry on … with a view of the other side

My Prayer for Us All

With a connection to a Divine Source, as you define it.
With an alignment with all that is glorious, as you know it.
With a unified front with our foundation at core ... may we always:

- Be surrounded with those who see our truest nature, not falling for our limited or negative view of self.
- Find "work" that serves our purpose as well as fills our pocketbook.
- Recognize our gifts and give them freely, without worry.
- Transcend a hectic and frantic world to hear the silent hum of a spiritual conspiracy at play.
- See through the illusion mask worn by the weary and scared, to see the reflection of another brother or sister on their chosen path.
- Reach out to the fallen, lend a hand to the hurting, give an ear to the heartbroken.
- Build bridges towards those who build walls before us.
- Be open to receiving after all that we have gifted to others.
- Take a break from the tasks and duties and jobs, in order to see the beauty before us.
- Set out on adventures around the globe, around the country or around the block – excited for the next new character and next new setting on this "world's stage."
- Find humor and levity when it can save the day ... and save a soul.
- Be who we are ... ever-growing and effervescent.

This is my prayer today. Join me in it if you wish.

LOVE'S MOMENTUM

*I wrote this prose in June 2019 after recollecting a peak experience of awakening
I had one day 20 years ago. It was 1999, and I was in a car with a girlfriend
and two of her young daughters, aged 6 and 10. The two girls were singing along
to the tune on the radio: "I Want It That Way" by the Backstreet Boys. For that
moment, in the sweet harmony of sisters, the innocence of pure love filled the
space. I was immersed in the full beauty of hearts free to express themselves.
Even today, upon reflection, I can remember how love demolishes the insanity
of this world of duality.*

Bursts of broken glass blow apart structures once sturdy
Cleansing from within the diseased, the downtrodden, the dirty
The peeling off of the dry and dead – reality's skin
Crushing the delusions of every place we've been
Laughable, all stress – in an instant – melts to the ground
An open sky – space brothers smile at what we've found
Celebration rumbles up from underground roots
The return of the Lord of Lords, the truth of truths
No more need for forgiveness, retribution, reparation
Nor the desperate propaganda to keep us all in separation
No longer preoccupied with agony's desire for attention
Forget that – here it comes – yes, it's love's momentum

It started from the first explosion of soul – a divine spark
Tumbling earthbound for the joyful excursion into the dark
Duality dripped upon us until we fell for it hook, line and sinker
Drowning our sorrows in poison – a lonely, early morning drinker
Buried in soot, buried in denial, barely a breath to exhale
Covered up – veil upon veil upon veil … upon veil
Even prayers leave us in despair, believing no one will ever be there
When all that is wanted is the face of someone, anyone, who cares

So we search – as we plunder, blunder, slumber along
Every step, deeper into the test, learning right from wrong
One hand clapping, our primordial face – all of life's conundrums
Will it come – where is the eternal, the source … love's momentum?

It is here, it is here, do not despair
Every time we proclaim that life is not fair
Seeds will bloom, given room, in full magic and splendor
Soothing all sores, healing all wounds … all so tender
Miracles arising everywhere – glimmering underneath dreams that are buried
The yin and yang, the feminine and masculine – forever married
Seen in anonymous donation, God's invisible helping hand
Seen in two young sisters, in sweet harmony,
singing glories of the latest boy band
Seen in the laughter of the child who recalls not history's hell
Seen in in secret response to prayer from our own wishing well
Seen in the dramas and karmas playing out in divine detail
Seen in the transcendent lesson gifted us every time we fail
Seen in the light of our life that often eludes our worldly attention
It is here, it is here, it is here … look for it … love's momentum

WHERE DO WE GO?

One day recently I thought to myself: "What could I share that would be of interest to others and what could carry a potential uplift?" Immediately my mind opened, and I felt this familiar sensation whenever inspiration meets me in the middle. My next questions: "Where do I go when I get creative?" "Is there some surreal inner world?" The response came to me in the piece of poetry here.

Where do I go when I hear the call
When the silent voice whispers my name, sweetly
Nudging me, nudging me, nudging me, gently
Awake
Aware now to a message floating to me like a feather dropped from heaven
Where does my mind and heart and soul go
Climbing white stairs without effort – a boost from behind,
a lift before me – upwards
And then a burst of energy, a smile, eyes closed
Knowing the words will appear in a feat of magic,
through that masterful magician
Not me, not me, no not me … no
Some other being – who meets me – in the place where we both can go
Where do I go?
When deserts arise on the horizons, bleak
Bringing desperation, heat, hunger, thirst
When the network programming news programs the worst
When a cry out to friends results in a lonely voicemail
Unanswered
When a fight breaks the silence, leaving us both alone
Once more
Where does my mind, my hear and my soul go?
No longer buoyant, hopeful – broken wings, cannot fly
Lost at sea, floating helpless, looking upwards, wondering why
In the end – nothing above and nothing below

Where can I go?
Where can I go – sitting at the bottom of a darkened pit
Hands grasping onto slippery mud that slides down walls, unscalable
Where can I go in this state of disrepair, unholy, ungodly
Eyes dimmed, light dimmed, hope dimmed
Where is there to go?
Where do we go?
Now
Now
Looking up – no longer asking why, no longer wanting to die
But just a desire, a longing, a prayer to return
Humble
Open
A beginner's mind that need not even begin to understand
The mystical, magical, invisible, outstretched hand
Listen, listen, listen … again
Being still … and knowing
Ever since the genesis of time, ever since grace's fall
Where I go when I hear the call
Where I go when I hear the call

THE TOPS OF TREES

I tried to imagine what the perception would be from the vantage point of spirit.
It's actually pretty nice.

It's all happening down here
The dance of destruction, dismay and fear
Landing, standing on the ground
Look at what we've found
Spinning, spinning, spinning around
The Earth, for what it's worth
Is your home of mayhem or mirth
We often perceive the darkness, downtrodden and disease
When we forget the view from the tops of trees

The roots crawl deep as we fall asleep
Bypassing the blessing and bliss
And an angel's everlasting kiss
The feathers blow, chaotic, to the wind
Losses overshadow every win
Can we please begin?
Not just seeing what the devil and demon sees
But rather that which nests in the tops of trees

The tops of trees
Will we ever see?
What must we believe?
And who must we be?
To finally see
The tops of trees

Yes, our opportunity is here
Disengaging from the taste and temptation of fear
We start a new and fanciful dance

We climb up … like a kid … branch by branch by branch
Like a kite or a bird
Or the truth found in word
Nothing too absurd
To take us to the very tippy top
Needing more than a skip, a jump or a hop
Above the roots, up the trunk
Distractions and delusions – all have shrunk
We ascend the tree, higher ever higher
Embracing the courage of performers atop high wire
A belly full of fire
To the supreme pinnacle, we now can perceive
And fly ever skyward over the tops of trees

The tops of trees
We rarely ever see
Not from our vantage view
Stuck in what we do
The tops of trees
We rarely see
A higher point above
A landscape of light and love
The tops of trees
We can finally see
We can finally see

THE SUN SHINES

A pal was talking about how he wanted to simply have positive impact by being himself, but not be attached to who is impacted in any certain way. I was thinking how the Sun shines and doesn't dictate how anyone receives its rays, as if it could say, "You over there get a tan, and you over there – receive some Vitamin D." No ... the Sun just shines.

The Sun shines, it shines, it's all it ever does
The Sun's identity – all it is and all it ever was
Remains ... it remains ... never restricted or restrained
Never lessoned, never censored, never detained
No matter day or night in some other distant land
No matter what astronomers come to understand
No matter clouds that come to block radiant rays
No matter the history found in the ancient of days
The Sun shines, it shines, though planets may make their move
There is no need to justify, no one to convince, nothing to prove
The Sun shines

Also not detained or restrained, there is another that remains
Right there, at your own center ... your love is the same
No matter the bitter blows that arrive in this mystery show
No matter the barriers and roadblocks that come and go
No matter the manipulation of mind, the raping of souls
No matter the gradual deterioration, or the moss that grows
It is there to be known, to be expressed, not repressed
Even if distress covers the light with a murky and muddy mess
Your love shines, with no need to impact or impress
But simply because at your genesis, you were blessed
The love shines

And so it is – from the beginning of eternity and beyond
A divine union created from the one sure bond

No need for magic wand, just a magician with a miracle to bring
A path you veered from, a song you forgot to sing
But it is not ever truly lost, it cannot be
As long as you have a heart longing to be free
As long as your soul is intact, at the center of your self
As long as love's warmth allows the hardened ice to melt
As long as every lie you learned is released into mist
Making way for the light that illuminates you in eternal bliss
The Sun shines
The Sun shines

SECOND NATURE

I wrote this for a female friend who said she had to get out into nature routinely to rediscover her own nature. This is for anyone who must go out into the woods every now and then to find themselves.

Into the woods, away from the noise
The innocence of girls and boys
Searching for beauty, the one true goal
A reminder of her very own soul
On the trail, through the brush
Strolling along, there is no rush
An eagle above, a squirrel, a bee
A stream to the right, a bended knee
Rushing by in effortless flow
This is home, here she'll know
The return to a garden, the eternal one
An inner nature, second to none

Second nature
Second nature
As simple as a second nature

A song for you, her dear forest home
It is here that she is never alone
Climbing a tree, looking down
The entire globe curving round
A far-off lake comes into view
Arising in mind, the old and the new
A landscape life on canvas art
A lifelong story from the very start
The mirror pool, reflecting like film screen
Movie magic, scene after scene after scene

The return to a garden, it's just begun
An inner nature, second to none

Second nature
Second nature
As sure as a second nature

As an infant babe, a mobile zoo
Talking by the time she was two
Getting back up after falling down
The playground fun, merry-go-round
Games in the park, a playful heaven
Yet, nature spirits said goodbye at seven
Reeling and rolling, dodging bullies at school
Half the time trying to play it cool
Teen years became the lean years
Measurements, grades, judgments, fears
Graduating to jobs, freeways and cement
A purpose, a plan – why was she sent?
Through the static and chaos, she's been lost
Success in the world of form – at what cost?
Around and around the entire globe curves
Is belonging to nothing what she deserves?
Nay … into the woods, away from the noise
The innocence of girls and boys
The bee, the squirrel, the eagle soaring above
Connection, unity, oneness … love
The yearn for the garden, the infinite Sun
An inner nature, second to none

Second nature
Second nature
As pure as a second nature
Second nature

TOUCH THE SKY

When the soul truly goes for it, I imagine the sky is the limit.

Moving within
Looking for the intention beyond the sin
A place to begin
And never look back
With eyes forlorn
Full of scorn
Agony born
No no no
The journey towards the present
Not the future, the bygone, or a time before
The deepest core
That very first hallway through that very first door
The first pen to paper establishing our story
Unveiling the romance, not the horrific or gory
The source of courage, guts and glory
Searching, searching ...
Our genesis, our start, our true foundation
The origin of heart seen in deep meditation
Seeking a simple act of restoration
Seeking, seeking ...
To be new again
As we move within
Atoning for any sense of sin
So far we can fly
As we let past and future die
As we touch the highest of the high
And rest in knowing – we can touch the sky
Touch the sky

HELLO FRIEND

I was watching an online yoga class when a pet cat came onto the screen, walking right up to the teacher. In sweet salutation, the teacher greeted her friend. Ah, relationships in their many forms … how shall we greet them today?

A cat meanders through the door during a yoga class
A dog approaches you on the couch, paws upon a lap
On a stroll outside, a hummingbird speeds by through the air
A trip to the zoo, every imaginable creature living there
Sharing a globe with the animals, in the wild and in the pens
The depth and beauty of a boy's and girl's best friend
Hello friend, hello friend
How are you today, how have you been?

Oh, the grandeur of relationships … how shall we greet them today?
What words come to mind, what is there to say?
For the barista working hard to prepare that right drink for you
For the waiter and waitress placing orders for your chosen food
For the loved one in partnership, making this circle of love complete
For the man, woman and child simply passing by on the street
As in the beginning, and then all throughout life, until the end
As we hold this sacred heart – in order to offer, share, heal or mend
Hello friend, hello friend
How are you today, how have you been?

How are you? What is new? What can we do?
With this life – to make it matter, to make it real, to make it true?
We welcome the morning, with a bow, a prayer, a knowing nod
We embrace the Universe, the angels, the spirit guides, and God
As in the myriad of classic books we store upon the shelves
We see within others as we see within ourselves
Husband, father, son, mother, daughter, wife
If you lived strictly on your terms, you may have missed out on life

Yet if you found the free, dancing energy encircling, you were indeed blessed
In-between the give and take: a mind at peace, a soul at rest
There is nothing that can make this existence any clearer or dearer
Than learning to appreciate, love and honor the one looking back in the mirror

And so, what words come to mind, what is there to say?
Ah, the wonder of relationships … how shall we greet them today?
The pets, the patrons, the clients, coworkers, bosses and more
The random humans we bump into at the soccer field, bank or store
The ones who have held us up as perfect, and the ones who made us all wrong
The inner self that has beaten us up for so long
The ones who challenged us, the ones who made everything a flow
A dear friend dog or a cat … peeking around a corner … hello
We faithfully take a stand for a totality of life we can finally defend
As we reframe everyone as companion, searcher, child of God and friend
How are you today, how have you been?
Hello friend, hello friend
Hello friend, hello friend

Family Matters

Often when you have arrived "home," you experience a sense of family, be that a spouse, children, parents, or those special friends who are so close they have entered that inner circle of a sacred tribe.

The heart is there.

For this chapter, I bring to the forefront those poems that reveal these family members. This even includes a poem written for my nephew's son Elijah who had yet to make his appearance, save for a gender reveal of blue confetti before both parents.

FAMILY MATTERS

*Everyone has an experience of family in one way, shape or form, and it can range
from the horrible to the transcendent. All in one day.*

However you define it, however you make it so
Here is the home … in which we all must grow
From seeds sewn to the bloom of majestic tree
However you guide it, however you want it to be
This is your family, be it close-knit or disjointed
From day one, from birth, you were anointed
You were gifted with the members who would create your clan
This was, once upon a time, the grace of a divine plan
Though visions may have been dashed, and memories shattered
Here is what really counts … here is how family matters

They push upon your boundaries; they imprint upon your soul
They take turns playing parts, as if cast in a theater role
Articulating impeccably, they recite the exquisite lines
Saying the right and wrong things, at the right and wrong times
They challenge your beliefs; they hold you in high esteem
They erect towering barriers you must transcend to reach your dreams
They may disappear without notice; yet for you they will arise and defend
Yes, as blood is thicker than water, they are ever-present in the end
Dissolving delusions of separation in its wake, strewn now in tatters
Here is the true value … here is where family matters

And so, with an epic flash of brilliance, a family held in highest view
Turning round and round and round, a global village ever new
In an embrace that encompasses totality, taking the most sacred stand
The largest circle – encircling the Earth – a family of woman and man
Can we expand that far, can we go to the depths of this reality?
Can we correct our insane minds, can we hold that much sanity?

It is for this collective, we take a moment and recognize who we are
Born again, returning once more, to a light that has never been far
However you define it, however you make it so
Here is the home … from which we all have grown
Where every nightmare ends, where every lurking shadow scatters
Here is the ultimate perception … here is why family matters

FOREVER MEMORIES – FOR MOM

For my mom, and all the memories that come with a lifetime with her.
Happy to have been able to give this to her in the living years.

Times on the lawn playing catch with this boy
Hot wheels and crazy wheels and all of those toys
Christmas tree lit with the remaining lights off
Spraying pillows with stuff so I wouldn't cough
A flurry of wheezes and sneezes, a Band-aid and some Kip
"Gonna try again next fall; did you have a nice trip?"
Cribbage and hearts and gin and gin rummy
Rubbing hot stuff on a sore and sick, little tummy
Washcloths and barf baskets, 7UP and a cracker
Kindly, gently asking, "Hey there, what's the matter?"

I simply want to remind you
Of just some of the reasons why I love you

Blasting air into necks with that motorboat sound
Bridge night meant we had to not be around
Spaghetti and Tuna Fish, Meat Loaf, Mac and Cheese
"Can I just stay up a little later – oh pretty, pretty please?"
Sea World, Magic Mountain and Disneyland after 4
Bob Newhart, Carol Burnett and some Mary Tyler Moore
Screams down the hall, "Don't make me come in there"
Not correcting it when Dad thought to cut my long hair
5-pitch and tennis, flag football and soccer
Sister saying, "Stop him" – and me saying, "Stop her"

I simply want to remind you
Of just some of the reasons why I love you

Tracing pictures on the oven, the day before it was due
Bringing bags in from the car was the hardest thing to do

Cindy's and Carrows and Cocos and Jon's
Apple Appeal and Blinkeys, the bowling alley and Vons
Laughing at trick-or-treaters; we didn't get the door
Thanksgiving dinner by the TV – "Hey Dad, wha¬t's the score?"
Dr. Grubel and St. Edwards, Father Clay and the rest
Turning this home into a haven, a sweet momma bird's nest
You were there through it all – the great mother of this clan
Holding it together, keeping us together – all part of God's plan
Do you remember what has happened in a time from before…
Where the memories are like guardians to an ever-open door

I simply want to remind you…

IT'S GREAT TO BE ALIVE – FOR DAD

Written for my dad – born February 28, 1928 – for his 90th birthday. He would stay so youthful and aware. He credited meditation and a belief in the power of the mind. I'm sure it wasn't the diet of fruit cups and Eggos.

And so the sentiments are clear; the affirmation set
Knowing what we put out there is what we will ultimately get
Recalling glimmers of visuals out of the murky haze
Holding close to heart all of our previous nights and days
Dreams of the past and future, memories of a life
"The Universe is perfect – it's great to be alive"
Coming into focus, names of yore from so far back
George Coulton, George Hutchings, Norm Zauchin, Jerry Kanack
Ricky Smith, Dick Sullivan, John Tyson, Marc Reymont
Friends and family – what more could anyone really want?

History: born in Detroit, father James and mother Mary
Sisters Amy and Barbara, later came the military
A reluctant student of economics, still you passed the test
Then came the unlikely insurance – it even took you out west
But first came destiny, God's good grace, fortune and luck
All from a stapler in a drawer … it was stuck
A vacation, the same weekend, taken together
A marriage – July 31, 1954 – that would last forever
1959 Redondo, 1962 Cambay Lane – following the road traveled less
Mary Lynn, Jimmy, Kathy, Emily, Monique, Emmett, Grace and Tess
Christmas mornings – waking up to half-eaten cookies on the hearth
Lawrence Welk, Hee Haw, Mary Tyler Moore, Carol Burnett and Bob Newhart
Slurpees, Jack in the Box balloons, McDonalds, Cocos, Carrows
Skinny Buffet, Apple Appeal, Jon's, Tijuana Tacos, Sambos
Japanese Dear Park, Santa's Village, Mt. Wilson, Jungleland
Sea World, Knott's Berry Farm, Magic Mountain, Wild Animal Park, Disneyland

All the places, every summer, in and out of traffic, where we've been
Familiar stories told over and over ... and over again
Meditation in the 70s, circle star one thousand and three ... relax
Farmers Insurance, claims and fraud, each and every photostat
Coming home with boxes, angry at the ringing phone while "on call"
Concerned over sniper fire at the front door and protecting us all
JFK, Coast to Coast, Art Bell and mystic Dollee
Doing the picks, bags of scratch offs, the winning lottery
Prairie Home Companion, Celtic Thunder, cassette tapes, ON TV
Bowling balls, bags, leagues, tournaments, and trophies
The carwash donuts, Black Panther fireworks, the "Family Pack"
Ragamuffin, Cosworth, Nicky, Rags, Fidrych, and Lucy the cat
Dan Meade over for football, the Miracle on Manchester game
The Rams always losing to the Vikings in bad weather – so lame

Long drives in the car, everyone asleep but me in the back seat
The habit you had of cleaning your ears with a car key
Cooking chicken noodle soup all the way to the end
Super Bowl VII, in 1967 and 1973 the trips to Michigan
Since I was sick, you took me to a store to get sherbet and some pop
Once got me a Dodger t-shirt after collecting those Pepsi soda tops
The amazing homerun by Kirk Gibson – man, what a shock
A call from Bete, those late-night metaphysical talks
Each memory – a gift from a surreal world, so sublime
Tears when Mary Lynn left home that very first time
Yes, visions of the past, present and future, memories of a life
Remembering always: the Universe is perfect ... it's great to be alive

ELIJAH WILL DECIDE

This was written for my nephew's son prior to his birth, as Elijah was taking his time in choosing the date of his arrival. Mom Amy and Dad Emmett at least knew of his gender with all the blue confetti.

The dawning light belongs to nature's will
The dusk at night echoes a silence, still
The wind ushers through the valley, a faint wisp
Planets align whenever eternity calls for eclipse
The muse cups an ear and whispers the call of love
The Divine discards fear with an expansive view from above
Flowers bloom, gardens blossom – all in the right time
Trees stretch skyward, a destiny they are sure to find
A womb cradles the sacred seed of life inside
The day of arrival? Yes, Elijah will decide
Elijah will decide

The underlying intention is clearly made
Worry not, worry not; do not be afraid
There is enough of everything that we could ever need
For he is born from the infinite, that miracle sacred seed

The choice made with voice – it carries us home anew
When it comes the time to act, we'll know just what to do
For those walking in the wilderness, knowing not where to begin
Will point in the right direction, turning their hearts back again
Taking a stand with hand in hand we'll heed the flowing tide
The direction? Which way? Yes, Elijah will decide
Elijah will decide

And so, we surrender once more, again, for the sake of all
And know we will arise when the Lord comes to call
As with the transitions: fall, winter, summer, and spring
And the everlasting song, as the chimes of freedom ring
The clock on the wall just knows the moment to strike
The shepherd cares for a flock … mother, sister, father and brother alike
A family gathered in symbolic circle, pointing towards the one
In timeless anticipation of eternity … finally begun
Open to the miracle, open with nothing left to hide
The day and time of our rebirth? Yes, Elijah will decide
Elijah will decide
Elijah will decide

The World's Latest Arrival

My niece Grace and her husband Cody, first time parents.
I wrote this on July 30, 2020, the day of Abigail's birth.

Well welcome here – welcome to this world
7 pounds 1 ounce – a healthy baby girl
So happy to see you, happy you came along
10 fingers and toes, almost 20 inches long
Born July 30, 2020, 2:10 in the afternoon
Right on time – truly not too late … and really not too soon
Gosh – what will be your story, your fairy tale?
Sweet little one … sweet Abigail

Your folks are so happy, smiles ear to ear
The world's latest arrival – so precious and dear
The sky opens up; pathways stretch ahead
Memories of the infinite fill the heart instead
The marriage of your spirit has caused you to create
An extension of your love, destined to fulfill a fate
Born amidst harmony, among those cradling peace
Here comes the grand celebration of a great, great niece

So what have you in store, any wonderful plans as yet?
I'm sure you'll be funny and sunny, with gags you'll give and get
Of course, it's all wide open; it will ultimately be up to you
Everywhere you'll go, and all you'll see and do
Of course, there will be the pratfalls, you know, those times to stumble
If anything like your parents, you'll be gracious, generous and humble
There need be no opposition; there is no need for rival
For you, newcomer here, the world's latest and greatest arrival
Gee – a lovely start to your journey, on into this chosen world
Born just this afternoon – a beautiful baby girl
Yes … what will be your story … your holy fairy tale?
Sweet little divine one … sweet Abigail

She Will Be in our Arms Regardless

*My wife and I invited my niece Grace and her husband Cody to our
10-year wedding anniversary on Zoom. Grace was committed, even if she had to
be holding her newborn Allison in her arms. So sweet.*

As we planned out a long-distance video call
We wanted to make sure we could see everyone
We didn't want to miss out an anyone at all
But naps come to those who are routinely under one
Yes, dear Allison only two months, would need to come along
We'd have Grace, her husband Cody, and little Abigail in tow
Leaving anyone out would simply be so wrong
Family connections are forever, for those you really know
For these are timeless moments that we'll always want to keep
Great niece Allison is innocent, pure, small, and harmless
She will be there, whether wide awake, fidgety, or asleep
Says Grace, "She will be in our arms … regardless"

She will be in her arms regardless the time and the day
She will be there if she yawns, naps or cries
She will be there most likely with nothing much to say
But with a sweetness whose limit is the infinite skies
For babies, kids and children of God are simply made this way
At core, we shimmer and shine in a surrendered state, defenseless
Just like Allison, we've been blessed by the Divine this and every day
Grace says, "She will be in our arms … regardless"

Now I imagine there is another type of world
One that does not recall the miracle of love
Forgetting the innocence of the little boy and girl
Never looking towards a high heaven above
It is filled with heartache, rage, guilt, and sorrow
Darkened by despair, deceit, and disconnection

Tragic is the manifestation from enmity and ego
Awaiting the depth of release that comes from reflection
Wandering around in the forest of folly, the grand delusion
There we are lost; it is sad, separate, and senseless
But underneath the layers, we can find the true solution
Yes … says Grace, "She will be in our arms … regardless"

So, rest assured lonely travelers, you can discover the path
From the eternal ocean, all drops of water shall reside
Fishers of men, the line has been surely cast
No longer can your illumination be set aside
You are invited, with an everlasting invitation, to the timeless call
To a haven priceless, heart-filled, humble, defenseless
No one will ever, ever, ever be missing at all
For Grace reflects the truth: "She will be in our arms … regardless"

My Momma Will Walk Again

I wrote this in February 2013 prior to my mother's passing when she was still bedridden. She used to claim that her immobility made her "just a blob." That was so sad to me. She passed in July 2014, into a freer realm beyond the physical.

I silently watch as my mother rests in her bed
Made to soothe and comfort, and lift her when need be
It makes it easier on her hip and her head
It makes it easier on her suffering knees
I quietly watch in agony believing she's never coming back
I find no words to speak, there's no place to hide
Invisible enemies of the past I plan to attack
Then surrender to the loss and the longing inside

I know it's not the start
I pray it's not the end
In dreamscapes and within my heart
My momma will walk again

My mother will stand up and walk once more
She'll effortlessly glide from room to room
She'll walk towards and then out that front door
She'll marvel again at the stars, the Sun, the Moon
She may even skip or dance or run for a bit
She'll be able to plant flowers in her own garden
Then … in its splendor … simply kneel down and sit
Yes, my momma will walk again

I know it's not the start
I pray it's not the end
In dreamscapes and within heaven's heart
My momma will walk again
My momma will walk again

Beyond the polarities of the loss and the win
Beyond the cruelties of sickness and sin
Beyond the need for a next of kin
Beyond the conversations we never did begin
Beyond the missed celebrations that should have been
Beyond the pain that all of us are in
In the peace and love found only within
In God's sweet embrace of an eternal heaven
In a timeless dream-state I long to live in
My momma will walk again
My momma will walk again
My momma will walk again

For My Wife – Kiss, Kiss, Kiss

Jennifer and I married on April 7, 2013. Our first date was July 17, 2010, with the proposal coming along exactly two years later. An obvious special date. In fact, we have a few anniversaries, all a benchmark of a love worthy of many poems.

For years, we have practiced a ritual of kissing three times, three times in a row. Yes, if you are doing the math in your head, that would be a total of nine. It's just something we do for the sake of affection.

This chapter hopefully captures that affection through a handful of specifically chosen pieces, all part of the sacred journey of the two becoming one.

THE MOMENT

*Sometimes you can drill down in time to find that moment when the shift turns
towards eternity. To think: for my wife and me, it involved us meeting up when
we both worked for the same public speaker, when I held this quasi
Vice-President position … as well as a silly movie.*

There was a moment, captured in time
When we went beyond the surface, into the sublime
Beyond simple "friends" who would hang out for fun
Into the realm of relationship, a pathway begun
Into the stratosphere, the sky now the limit
We were there to surrender, now in it to win it
Could there be a single moment, captured like this?
Initiated with a movie, a couch and a kiss

It wasn't about that movie, not a teaser nor a thriller
It was actually quite boring, and it starred that guy Ben Stiller
It was all about the buildup – from our first meeting day
Through the pickup at the airport and the Sheraton on the bay
Through the non-profit event that showed my short film
Through the first time you asked, "Who is this Vice Prez Jim?"
Through the Indian dinner, me taking a samosa home
Through all of those e-mails and a few chats on the phone
Who knew it would lead to an anniversary such as this?
Initiated with a movie, a couch and a kiss

But yes, it sure did, we would move on from there
Into a realm of inclusion, consideration and care
A Bible verse or two, the ones we wanted to read
When two or more are gathered, where could it all lead?
The joy that we had as we explored a wonderland
Getting as close as we dared, as close as we can

Funny to look back on a moment not to miss
Initiated with Ben Stiller, a couch and a kiss

And so here we are and, yes, here we go
On with the movie, on with the show
Plenty of samosas to eat and hot chocolates to drink
Cheering on the Kings and Dolphins, even when they do stink
Walking and talking, the trips up and back from LA
Meet the players, Hockeyfest, some games and 5ks
Overcoming the challenges that have kept us at bay
So we can shine ever brighter, as we greet each new day
Great abundance is here now – health and wealth – all of this
To think it all started – with a movie, a couch and a kiss

EVERY DAY IS JULY 17

My wife and I had our first date and our proposal date two years apart, to the day. The proposal was pretty unique – a treasure hunt throughout our favorite places, each holding a Scrabble tile that would ultimately spell out "WILL YOU MARRY ME." Umm, she said "yes."

A date to celebrate on the calendar
As we navigate the turbulent seas day by day
As we move about the landscape of life
As we take the unstable trails along pathway
Every morning a chance to wake up to abundance
Every day moments into the wind we can lean
Every evening a time to put our troubles to bed
Every day is July 17

A day we can recall a memory of taking the plunge
A day to make a pledge for the one pure connection
A day to snuggle and cuddle if we so choose
A day to fall into sweet and serene affection
A day we move along to yet another level
A day we can take a daily walk, regardless of the weather
A day we can cross lines to move ever higher
A day we can find the time to play together
A day we can watch our drama, upon the couch or off
A day we can be surprised about what it all can mean
A day we make sure to be present for each other
Every day is July 17

We can take our journey for fun, for laughs, for gaffes
We can make an adventure finding clue upon clue
In life's crazy zigzagging scavenger hunt
We'll see just what we can find, just what we can do

We can plan for a future aligned with the one power
We can propose a commitment at oceans' sacred scene
In a setting where waves crash gently upon the shore
Every day is July 17

So, as we celebrate one calendar date
Upon trails we follow faithfully so we can find our way
Navigating the seas and exploring mighty landscapes
We can make July 17 … every day

THE SACRED ALTAR

Written for our wedding day April 7, 2013, Point Loma, the Thursday Club.
The plaque with this poem was present at the edge of our center table.

For, we come to the sacred altar …

Where archangels arrive to bless
A lifelong journey finding its rest
Where ceremony poetically weaves a tapestry
And garment, ritual and prayer join in majesty
Where supportive souls travel distance to stand as witness
To the magic, to a miracle, to the source of all such kindness
To the dance acknowledging unimagined connection
To the couple uncovering life's sweet affection
Where there is no longer excuse for the failure or the falter
We come – open, surrendered, free – to the sacred altar
To the sacred altar…

Joining with angels and guides – the guardians of the fate
Realizing in God's time, there is no "too early" nor "too late"
We stand here – side by side – dreaming in one direction
Yearning for awakening through the glorious resurrection
The journey – a million slip-ups, sidesteps and trips along the way
Every one of them guiding us gently towards today
So that we may know, and we may say –

Thank you dear mystery, dear heart of hearts
May everything we've been through please play a part
In the realization of all that ever mattered
Where two or more are forever gathered
The holy ones – the sister, brother, mother, father
For all of us, indeed, we come to the sacred altar
To the sacred altar …

No longer lonely individuals lost in a forest of our own making
No longer shipwrecked sailors downtrodden with masts breaking
No longer bitter travelers with feet blistered, bleeding and sore
No longer desert dwellers left thirsty, starving for more and more
We look towards the mysterious presence that cares, truly, for us
In the spirit of unspeakable, unknowable, unprovable trust
We need only true perception to show us the forgiven path
It is our salve, our guidance, our treasured map
Where there is the third entity to guard and guide as we go
Where the surrender to the highest is what makes it so
Where there is no longer the roadblocks of failure or falter
We come – on this holy and blessed day – to the sacred altar
We come … to the sacred altar

Into Eternity I Enter

Written for Jennifer. It is my hope, though you may not know each specific reference, these selected memories bring forth a subtle recognition at the level of the heart.

Memories arrive at the front door of my mind
A lake's eternal rippling rings, the echoes of time
Did we ever really part ... from that very first union?
Did we ever really start ... was there need for reunion?
Was there ever a moment, where our souls did not show?
Was there a time, of your splendor, I did not know?
Was there ever a struggle of conflicting give and take?
Or did we simply surrender to the One ... for God's sake?
Oh no, lines blur for the true receiver and sender
It is at this time ... into eternity I enter

Memories arrive at the front door of forever
It's as if we have always been here together
Memories of absolute glee, bouts of deep and lasting laughter
Lombardy trophies and Stanley Cups we went after
Wild rides through the sexual landscape of adventures
Vegas, Magic Mountain, Knotts, a cruise with World Ventures
Ammachi, Victoria BC, Indian food in Big Bear
Countless oils, remedies, and meals ... given with your care
Freedom For All, 1000 Breaths, engaging gatherings ¬ at the home
A wedding or two for the committed, never to be left alone
A vow and ceremony would burst forth a new birth
Saying goodbye, for now, to some we knew on this Earth
On mystical levels, on walks and talks, we will always be
With that regal, smarty-pants one we know as Hennessy
In your yoga, we find shanti, namaste and our truest center
It is at this time ... into eternity I enter

For here we are – two solar systems searching for the sacred star
And to think, at no time, did we ever have to travel far
The path was created by the Divine, we simply found our way
And even through upset, stress, and fear, we will not stray
Led through your giving, your sharing, your sweetness, your beauty
A true heart, a true love, a real blessing, a real cutie
The practical one whose deep waters run romantic
Echoed through this poet's wordsmithing semantics
Long ago, or in this eternal moment, we made a choice
To follow a Christed direction and the angel's loud voice
A couple, riding the waves, in tandem, in communion
Removing ourselves from dim caves of darkness and delusion
So, did we ever really start … was there really a reunion?
Did we ever really part … from that very first union?
Will there ever be a place, where our spirits do not go?
Will there ever be a time, of our light, we do not know?
Nay, we follow the echoes of time, the ripples on the surface lake
We fall into the arms of the One … for God's sake
Yes, we make the smart move, into the sweetest of sweet surrender
As we awaken and realize, at this time … into eternity we enter

WINNIE THE POOH & YOU

It was Jennifer's birthday, and I just had to find a way to bring in the voice of her favorite pal Winnie the Pooh. I figured I could simply channel the silly ole bear. It was helpful that when I squeeze the belly on her stuffed animal "Pooh Bear," he speaks the line: "A very large pooh bear hug would be nice about now."

Well here we are, just me and you
Doing just what we two can do
The gang is here in the Hundred Acre Wood
Doing the things that all of us should
Piglet and Owl and Kanga and Roo
Eeyore and Rabbit, Christopher Robin too
All of us should simply take a bow
A very large pooh bear hug would be nice about now

This is from Winnie, the one known as Pooh
Doing the things that I can do
Asking questions and remembering fun
The loving embraces, the honey run
I hope I don't get stuck when I go for food
"Oh bother" – that is the extent of my attitude
I just want to walk with you in the spirit of "wow"
A very large pooh bear hug would be nice about now

A very large pooh bear hug would be nice about now
It's what nice people and huggy people would come to allow
They are snuggly and wuggly and all of those things
It's what nice people and huggy people like to bring
To get one of those hugs would make me so lucky
Soft and warm, like the happiness of a warm puppy
So, let's make a promise, let us take a vow
And do one of those large pooh bear hugs right now

In the end, we shall walk, and we shall talk
In silence, in pondering, in picking up rocks
We'll make our way around all of the blocks
Going and going … until we decide to stop
Even when it's quiet we can hear each other speak
It's in the clouds and in the steps that we will reach
Hoping for no more ouches and no more ow's
A very large pooh bear hug would be nice about now
A very large pooh bear hug would be nice about now

WALKING THE DAILY WALK WITH YOU

With our 10-year anniversary at hand, I took the time to reflect on the walks my wife and I take every day.

Step after step, some slow, some swift, left and then right
Down Berry Street, east on Mt. Vernon, then south on McKnight
Looking for relief from the world of mankind, looking for love
We take our daily walk with nothing but the sky and clouds above
Passing trees and lawns, passing neighbors who oftentimes wave
Trying to process the junk and gunk of the working day
Beyond the retirement home stillness, beyond friendly Ricardo's
This is the path of least resistance; this is simply the way it goes
Sometimes in life, there really is nothing more to say or do
Walking the daily walk with you

Recalling different memories, my father's "It's great to be alive"
Down Berry Street, left on Mt. Vernon, then right on Gold Lake Drive
We walk against the wind heading west, but we do our best
An abandoned house, a barking dog or two, a grounded bird's nest
Planning future adventures – some bring agitation, some bring smiles
Another installment for our friendly cat visit for "The Nala Files"
Past the council member's manor, alongside school grounds and gravel
With mixed emotions … recalling the one missing on our travels
Sometimes in life, there really is nothing more to say or do
Walking the daily walk with you

Now over the years, there is a sacred stroll that we can recall
Embracing experiences from the first day, embracing it all
Our 10-year anniversary, April 7 it will be, so much we have seen
With so many walks and talks, and so many miles in between
For better or worse, we find the laugh in the gap, we enjoy the ride
For beyond the bless or curse, the Divine joins us there in stride

The path of least resistance; never to turn away or snub
It was there, Point Loma, Santa Barbara Street, the Thursday Club
When you walked the aisle, in front of family and God, the ocean view
Sometimes in a lifetime, there truly is nothing more to say or do
Walking the daily walk with you

Kiss, Kiss, Kiss

I couldn't have a chapter title with the words "kiss, kiss, kiss" without some explanation. This one was written for my wife – and our habitual trilogy of kisses to equal nine – in November 2023 as this manuscript was being completed.

The morning call, the breakfast ringing bell
A time to be still, where only time will tell
Serene is the setting; we are the couple that is cast
In a fleeting and temporary moment that will forever last
A wonderful meal, an appreciation with full embrace
Before the rest of the day and the world we must face
Right here, in a moment like this
The time is now – kiss, kiss, kiss

Upon departures, as life's crossroads take us away
There is a symbolic gesture that will always stay
A farewell wave, a reminder about items to bring
A checklist to ensure we both have everything
And then upon reunion, as the journey returns us again
We're back at square one, wherein the end, we can begin

Right there, in many moments like this
The time is now – kiss, kiss, kiss

And so it is, within experiences however they may come
We clasp and cuddle and caress, knowing infinity has begun
There is no future, there is no past, there is only now
Surrendering to the divine path and all the beauty it will allow
Out of reach of fear's temptation, beyond the wrong and right
When it's time to say hello, when it's time to say goodnight
Right in this instance, in an eternal moment like this
The time is here – kiss, kiss, kiss
Kiss, kiss, kiss
Kiss, kiss, kiss

For Our 4-Legged Friends

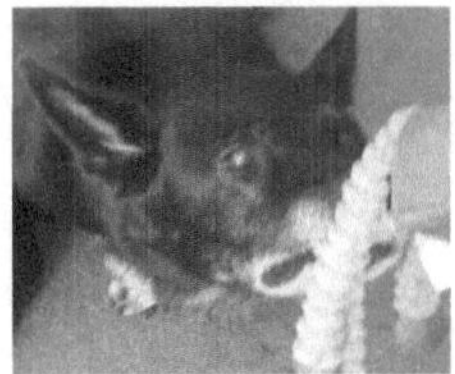

In sifting through the 275-plus poems that would constitute this *Breadcrumbs'* volume, I found a number of poems written for our pooch Hennessy, a special Akita mix that Jennifer rescued in 2006.

I also discovered some pieces that related to other 4-legged friends.

Along the journey, something would be amiss without the unconditional love of our dearly devoted, best furry friends.

AND I LOVE HER TOO

"Written By" Hennessy Simone Ellis, Akita Mix. Rescued by Jennifer from the Marin Humane Society, February 2006. A sentiment from Hennessy to Jennifer as imagined by this poet who chose to translate Hennessy's spirit and unconditional love into these words here.

She came to me
I came to her
She rescued me
I was saved for sure
I wrecked the washroom
Returned two times
I was sure to be doomed
I had crossed the lines
She took me in
How lucky I was
She knew where I'd been
She loved me ... just because

Just because I am who I am
Not because I've been where I've been
Not because I got scared when left alone
Not because I never really had a home
Not because I was a runt in a litter of nine
Not because I tore down the window blinds
Not because I scratched the front door
But ... because of the reason I did that for

I did it to be back with her
She was the one who saved me for sure
She was the one who cared when everyone else gave up
She was the one who cleaned my throw-up

She was the one who fed me even when I couldn't beg
Even mac-and-cheese, and some scrambled egg

Why does she like me?
I could make owners fret
Because as you can see
I am just a simple pet
I am a simple dog
I play like girls and boys
I can even be a hog
When it comes to my chew toys
She loves me
This is true
She loves me
And I love her too

She takes me for walks
So that I can pee
I train her to throw the ball
So I can run free
Then return to my bed
So I can curl into sleep
Resting my head
And dreaming of sheep ...
... And parks and hikes and quesadilla snacks
And walk-a-thons and visits and friend-time and baths
And car-trips and bank-trips and beach-trips galore
Finding any excuse to get out that front door
To do the things that we can do
To show all the reasons ... that I love her too

She loves me just because
She knows where I've been
How lucky I was
She took me in
I was saved for sure

She rescued me
My heart so pure
She came to me
An owner who only had one thing to do …
… And I love her too
… And I love her too

I Said Chloe's Name

Karen Pearlman loves her Cocker Spaniel Chloe. Everyone on Facebook knows this. On social media, I heard a story of how one of Karen's friends said Chloe's name during a church service, in prayer for better health. Though Karen has by now lost her dear friend, the prayers were present previously, as well as onward continuously.

It's who we are, it's how we live
I heard the news, I wanted to give
The social media post said your dear dog was ill
A prayer for all that is peaceful and still
As we join forces with the illumination of God's will
Into your cup, from divine abundance, we will fill
I went to the altar today, before the candle flame
Into the space, I said Chloe's name

I said her name so that all could wish the best
For her health, for her vibrancy, for her rest
I said Chloe's name, and it gave life to the word
The blessings of bounty, we can be assured
By a mere utterance, she was placed into the mind of God
That little rascal with dark curls, that wonderful dog
Healing any conditions, the aches, the owies and the pains
Glady, and with exuberance, I said Chloe's name

And so here we stand, as concerns shift to care
Of the path of heart and healing, we are aware
Perfect health in all its forms – spirt, body and mind
For those who remember the power of simply being kind
And giving to those in need when it's time to say a prayer
Standing strong in faith, as concerns shift to care
Surely yet humbly … happy that up to this alter I came
So that I could speak into the space … I said Chloe's name
I said Chloe's name

PRAYERS FOR DAISY

Some prose for my father-in-law Roger and his doggy Daisy, back when both were among the living.

We all have a Daisy.
We all love someone so much.
We all hold so deeply to the connection of a dear one.
This is a prayer for Daisy.
A prayer for her wellbeing, her health, her healing.
Yesterday, the word came from my father-in-law. His dear Daisy has been hurting with a troubled esophagus. And so we pray.
And we hold out for the best.
For we all have a Daisy.
A dear, soft, sweet spot in our heart where there is room for another.
It's as if how our loved one feels, we feel ... how our loved one is doing, we are doing.
It's not a co-dependency; it's a connection, an extension of our self with another self. It is our expanding to include the health of our dear one, be it a spouse, a child, a sibling, a parent ... a family pet.
Little Daisy – a faithful Boston Terrier – was located as a rescue by Roger a couple years ago.
Since then, they have been inseparable. A boy and his dog, no matter the age of either. If ever my wife and I receive a holiday card from my father-in-law, it's always signed "Dad and Daisy."
And so we pray.
For Daisy. For her full recovery.
Knowing that there is one power in this Universe. Not two powers, but rather one.
And this power is infinite in knowledge, peace, joy, abundance and health.
In that perfect state of health, we are all connected.
We know and accept that anything unlike this perfect state is released at this very moment.

And we are well.
Daisy's body is in pure alignment with oxygen flow and blood flow, enriching her entire body.
The unlimited source of energy is alive and well within her.
As it is alive and well within all those who have their own Daisy ... in their own life.
For this vision, we do give thanks, in gratitude.
As it is being made manifest right here, right now.
We let it go and let it be.
And so it is.
Amen.
And so it is, for my father-in-law and his pooch.
In a beautiful vision, no matter what the surface appearance displays.
In a time of need ... and connection.
In this prayer for Daisy.

RUN FREE

Another piece of prose for you dear reader. Do you ever see your dog while he or she is sleeping, with paws moving swiftly as if your pet is jetting around? It is precious.

My dog runs in her sleep.
Her little paws flipping up and down as she's lying there. Eyes closed.
Breathing deep.
She must be asleep.
And yet she runs.
It doesn't appear to be a sprint but maybe a simple graceful jaunt. A jog.
A trot.
And where could she be going? I wonder.
Could it be our neighborhood park next door? Could it be her going after a chew toy we threw down the hall? A run on the beach? She never seemed to like the water much.
Maybe she's recalling the time when she's ready for dinner and she jets to and fro between her momma and me hoping to get one of our attention.
One of ours anyway. Barking loudly.
For it's true – besides the flipping paws, every once in a while she'll eek out this little muffled huff. High pitched. So faint. It's actually sort of cute, but at the same time it's somewhat sad.
She's trying to communicate something to someone, and she's also moving along in stride.
I will listen, I tell her.
Whatever your little high-pitched huff is trying to say I will see if I can decipher. Wherever you want to run to, I can run with you. The beach? The park? For a stuffed animal?
I will go along.
With you.
As we run. As we jaunt. As we attempt to get someone's attention.
In our dreams.

A Dream of Tug of War

I had a dream of me and my dear dog Hennessy. It had me thinking of how much people could benefit from a game of tug of war which wasn't a war at all.

Yes, last night I dreamed of a tug of war
Between our dearly departed dog and me
Seemed so real, nothing less, nothing more
Just a visit from our dear Hennessy
I questioned what she wanted with this boy
I didn't know what she would bring
At last, she brought to me a toy
It was a fluffy, chewy, funny type thing
We lost our girl in 2021, you see
It was so deeply painful to the core
And now I'm left with just a dream
A dream of tug of war

She was the one who started the game
She pulled, and then shook from side to side
Of course, I played along just the same
No other option really but to oblige

She was always the one to offer up the prop
It was just her way to have me included
She had to have both her mom and pop
She was never one to have any fun excluded
She'd invite me on walks no matter the weather
She'd stand there planted, and stare at me
The whole pack had to be walking together
That was the way of Hennessy

So the tug of war, was it really a fight?
Or just a way to have some fun?
Was someone supposed to feel a slight
Or had play time just begun?
Surely, this was now a time to connect
To find that game we could play together
Full of mutual joy and mutual respect
How I wish it could last forever
But one dream ends and another begins
What is one to do when a goodbye is in the cards
Who cares who loses and who wins
Isn't life and all its losses already too hard?
For life is never what it really seems
Let us play the games and not be sore
Even though sadly, I'm left with just a dream
Just a dream of tug of war

Farewell

One of the more challenging aspects of a life-long journey is the experience of loss.

This chapter's poems are dedicated to the departed of loved ones and the love that will never be forsaken.

THERE ARE NO WORDS

Written for anyone who has experienced heartbreaking separation and loss. My wife and I experienced four immense losses in a six-month period of 2021: our Hennessy, my best friend from childhood and both of our fathers. Each will be forever missed, in words that cannot be truly conveyed … though I do my best.

This poet goes silent, the stage goes dark
The full-length soliloquy now reads stark
The moment is hush, like the eternal dawn
The lyrics may end … the music plays on
There's nothing to be said, nothing to be heard
Truth be known … there are no words

Thou shall not match the terms for love
As we rise to heights countless miles above
Any attempt at alignment becomes a breach
The utterance of language simply cannot reach
In the sky, only room for highflying birds
Truth be known … there are no …

There are no words for this kind of pain
Days and nights go by … again and again
There are no words for this sort of loss
The giving and receiving, the highest cost
There are no words for the heart that knows
The love that grows and grows … and grows

So, we shall be still tonight, and not give a thought
To the caves of shadows where we can get caught
We shall not try to understand that which goes beyond
But lie down in the field, and recall the dawn
Where we can say nothing more, but rest assured
Truth be known …

Hennessy – Come to Me

Sometimes, even if a pet has been gone for some time, there is the longing for a time before. Memories arise daily, from the game of firing dog food kibble into our Hennessy's mouth to my announcement of her kicking her hind legs after peeing with the silly phrase "keeek, keeek, keeek." It is all there in the memories as well as the longing.

We keep the toys that carry so many joys
With some, somehow, still making noise
Memories last beyond the distant past
Recalling how all of our characters were cast
Us in the front seat, you in the backseat
Surely, making every one of us complete
Words we'd repeat when we would meet
Touch, sit, catch, and keeek – keeek – keeek
Feeling free, bending down to a knee
Calling out your name, "Hennessy – come to me"

Left behind, a puzzle piece never to find
Forever missed, forever in our mind
Wanting to rewind, time and space are not kind
Reaching out for a mystic reading or a sure sign
We do not fear that the loving presence is here
It's just that the physical touch is not near
The journey of the daily walk, the two-way talk
Living without that is a devastating shock
They tell us to trust, I imagine that we must
Yet still calling out, "Hennessy – come to us"

So, we go our way, living onward day to day
Recalling beautiful memories on this – your birthday
How you'd never "stay" but like to tug-of-war play
Proceed to open gifts not sent to you, anyway

How you would frustrate when we would meditate
Through the door you would no longer hesitate
Perhaps beyond this plane, you will remain
Where we all three will remember our names
In dream-states and love-scapes free, we'll know where to be
Where maybe, just maybe, you will call out … "Come to me"

THE BIRTHDAY CARD YOU NEVER GOT

I have a friend who wished to clear away any issues with her mother by sending a specific birthday card. Within it, she worked so hard at sculpting some deeply caring sentiments. Sadly, she just missed. It would be a card that didn't make it to her mom before her passing.

Sent with love, care, and the call for connection
This would be a divine resurrection
Life, brand new, post reconciliation
A gift for you, dear Mom, in a pure communication

From daughter to mother, I wanted it right
Not too nasty, not too nice
Just to eliminate the bicker and the fight
To illuminate the way with dawn's early light

A peace offering – this is what I sought
Searching bin to bin – aha – a present … I bought
But as dreams sometimes crash, it was all for naught
It was the birthday card you never got

The call it came; it came yesterday
My brother said what he had to say
You were simply gone – all in one day
The card would arrive at your home anyway

The loss is intense, the anguish and the pain
It will never ever, ever, ever be the same
I had so many years to extinguish the blame
Now there is just a card, with an address, a stamp and a name

I'll have to say goodbye, ready or not
I feel I've been unfairly trapped or caught

In-between what I loved and what I fought
Now I simply watch the barriers break down and rot
It's what I know now; it's what life and death have taught
About a connection that never could be bought
Even in the birthday card you never got

FOREVER SIBLINGS

This one is for my friend Bryce, who lost his sister Marci in March 2009.
I received one of those Legacy e-mails about the anniversary of her death and
was inspired to offer some compassion.

I understand the anniversary has been rough on you in the past
But in the end, there's only one thing, one thing, that will forever last
That giddy excited smile, that exuberant and boisterous laugh
The infinite memories of countless moments that forever siblings have
As war heroes and dead politicians receive the glory of a flag half-staff
You will recall a surfer on the sea … you following along on your drifting raft
You will always be a member of a family, with characters divinely cast
You will always know the love that forever siblings have

Siblings know of a bond that lives beyond the spite and dares
Siblings are connected through an invisible thread of care
Siblings hold a connection that will forever be theirs

I understand it's easier as time and space give way
Though rust never sleeps, nor does corrosion and decay
Wishes do come true – as you wish you might, and you wish you may
Something below the surface will, in eternity, always stay
Underneath the sunbeams, we sunbathe, as down we will finally lay
A lone surfer, adrift on the ocean, returns from her ride on the waves
Nothing, in truth, can ever take this bright soul away
You will always know the love that forever siblings have today

Siblings know of a bond that lives beyond the spite and dares
Siblings are connected through an unconditional love and care
Siblings hold a connection that will forever … and ever … be theirs

THE REUNION – A POEM FOR MY MOTHER AND HER MOTHER

My mother passed in July 2014. Though 100 miles apart when it happened, I felt time and space stand still in the moment without even knowing what was taking place. I embraced the miracle of life and death and the idea my mother was met by her own mother at this fateful moment.

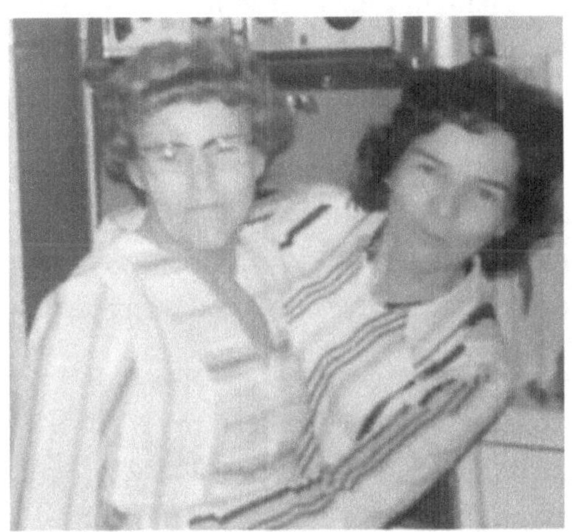

I know this to be true, as I know the Sun
I know it as sure as time has begun
Though time stood still for this here son
I felt the reunion that was sure to come
My mother and grandmother, they met once more
One stood for the other at the illumined door
In the heavenly heights, where only angels soar
This was the embrace grandma had waited for…

The reunion is here for all to share
The reunion is for those with the call to care
The reunion is home to everyone, everywhere

Unimagined joy for this here boy who only wished for her release
From the shackles and chains, the aches and pains that never seemed to cease
Holding out for the pure, merely wanting for sure the eternal path of peace
Happiness for my mom, kindly come along, I dearly begged God please
And it came to be, a miracle to see, this story I am writing
The beauty of souls who could take the stroll upon their reuniting
Ready to tell the tale – beyond success and fail – of a family uniting
I saw the end, within these forever friends, of the struggle and the fighting

The reunion is here for all to share
The reunion is for those with the call to care
The reunion is home to everyone, everywhere

When crisis calls in all of our falls, and safety is torn and tattered
And man and beast, none the least, is beaten down and battered
And we are scared, as in nightmare, our dreams are sliced and shattered
Finding in the end, with every mend, only kindness matters
Only kindness matters …

The message I would hear, it was so dear, my mother would send to me
Finding at last, awakening so fast, a vision I could not see
She came through song, I would sing along, her spirit flight so free
A precious jewel, goodbye to the cruel, hands building eternity
So if you are lost, at all cost, do come and seek what's yours
Just like my mother, all sisters and brothers can find illumined doors
Blasting past barrier, you'll be the carrier, beyond all ceilings and floors
Taking the trip, on your sacred ship, towards familiar shores

I know this to be true, as I know the Sun
I know it as sure as time has begun
Yet, time can stand still for everyone
There's always the reunion that is sure to come
For each enemy and ally, we shall meet once more
There's a guardian for each of us at heaven's door
An unlimited unity we all have in store
This is the embrace we've been waiting for…

The reunion is here for all to share
The reunion is for those with the call to care
The reunion is home to everyone … everywhere

SENDING AN ANGEL TO MY DAD

Written for my father, James Arthur Ellis – February 28, 1928 - March 15, 2021. I didn't know what else I could do but silently send support for safe and peaceful travels. And to write this.

What can you do when there's nothing you can do?
Where can you be when it seems you can't come through?
What can be accomplished when you're supposed to let it go?
What is there to know when there is no way to know?
What can be done when you give it up to the glory on high?
What can you trust so that you and family can get by?
When the love is bigger than any actions that can be taken?
When mortal time and space makes existence seem forsaken
What is there for me to do, when feeling downcast and sad?
Perhaps simply … sending an angel to my dad

Yesterday in hospital bed, he laid in wait
Vitals were good, but other signs not so great
The morning came, and the text gave harsh news
Now there was something I knew I had to do
Get on the wet and rainy road, as fast I could
Crystal clear, taking action, hoping for the good
As I drove, I still questioned what I could truly bring
Like the drummer boy, I didn't think I had anything
But focused on my mission, I brought what I had
Perhaps just a prayer and … sending an angel to my dad

Sending an angel
Standing tall as we must
Summoning the faith
Surrounding ourselves in trust

Arriving at the hospital, it was a surreal scene
Something you see on TV or movie screen
Nurses, hospital room, hospital bed
My father prone … and my sister gently touching his head
Memories, concerns and tears arrive in times of life and death
With my eyes closed, I barely noticed his last breath
What can one do in moments when there is nothing left to do?
When the immensity of love is all that can come through
Perhaps just be, stay calm, and remain in the presence
Rekindling what exists in the still eternal essence
Peace would come in knowing there would be nothing left to add
Just this poem and … sending an angel to my dad
Sending an angel to my dad

FROM THE SKIES

Janet Lundquist, a life-long skydiver, was a friend who battled cancer for over a decade. No, the cancer did not win. Anyone who got the chance to know her was the winner.

Far beyond this temporal time, high above this physical plane
There resides a reality no one can truly explain
Some say it is light-infused; it glimmers, it shimmers and shines
It embraces every single soul, leaving not one of us behind
It comes without concealment, without a hint of disguise
It comes from a sacred realm; it comes … from the skies

Though an unknown mystery, this haven we can endeavor to know
As we trek along life's winding road … as above, so below
Here on Earth, we knew a dear heart, a risk taker, a fun one
A highly engaged listener, so clearly present for everyone
Supportive, strong, generous, sweet, as any friend would want to have it
A one and only, positive personality, the gal known as "Dammit Janet"
She shall remain in heart, mind and soul, just as all angels shall arise
She may be seen in a piercing, panoramic view … from the skies

A woman of courage, a woman supporting transformation, a woman of action
A renaissance woman, freely following the wind and her own passion
A freelance photographer, jewelry maker, a fighter, a survivor
A sailor, pilot, hiker, pet-sitter, an eternal skydiver
The first tandem dive in 1984, near 5000 jumps, quite a rarity
Her competitive 8-way skydiving team – "Vertical Disparity"
Marrying Fred in 1995, a normal chapel wedding full of binding ties
The couple and 50 friends then made the reception; they dropped in …
from the skies

Upon Janet's transition, friends from the cyber cloud left their remarks
Wishing her safe travels on the journey, upon which she just embarked

Kim: We are all better humans because of her, she was love and light
Kate: You squeezed every damn drop of juice out of life
Wendy: Such grace and strength, with a smile on her face
John: An amazing influence back in the Reading Eagle days
Chad: She changed my views on life in many ways
Corliss: Michael is on the lookout … Jennifer: My heart hurts today
Sarah: Beautiful soul … Heather: A spirit warrior …
David: May you fly free forever more
Dressler: Fierce and funny and crazy and naughty;
she left it all on the dance floor
Jack: Always a forever smiling heart … Alex: Her love stays with us
Fred: She was sustained through the loving connections she created
with each of us
Sarge: Nature's gentle folk … Maddog: Always fun to be around …
Georgia: Gifted everyone's lives
Overall, for every person she touched, Janet is truly a gift … from the skies
From the skies

GOODBYE BEAUTIFUL

*I attended the funeral service for the lovely Lisa Kalison-Tota. Her husband
Attila told the story there, how she would not allow him to leave the house
without a kiss and a phrase shared between each other.*

She would not let you leave the house so fast
No, that just would not do
An emotion and an experience that was meant to last
A kiss from you to her … and her to you
She'd appeal to you as you took your leave
In a ritual so precious, so rich, so full
A chance to give, a chance to receive
After each kiss: "Goodbye handsome" … "Goodbye beautiful"

Such a custom came from a soul so pure
Not a demand, really, at all
She just wanted to make 100 percent sure
From the front door porch, she would call
You would of course grant her this wish
And return to her in a graceful deed
A kiss neither of you would want to miss
Fulfilling the sentiments of a sacred need
A gesture bringing closer the energy, the life
Mind to mind, lips to lips, eye to eye
The dance of unity, a husband and wife
A parting farewell, a beautiful goodbye

Now, since time has passed, and we have all lost our friend
The rituals turn to something more surreal
Signaling neither the beginning, nor even the end
We embrace a divine and timeless world so real

We've had to deal with the parting and the pain
Allowing grief and sadness to have its say
An experience for you, we could never really name
Providing a path for the truth, the light, and the way
Having to see the curtain come down one last time
Praying for a soul recognizing that which remains full
Reminding us all of a reality beyond the borderline
In an everlasting kiss: "Goodbye handsome" … "Goodbye beautiful"

HE WAS A FIGHTER

This was written for Russell Shatto, a man who had been through a lot of loss prior to taking his final leave in July 2014. A motorcycle accident in 1993 leaving him legally deaf was just one of the battles he faced. So was the brain tumor, which would be his last fight.

From the beginning and until the end
He was a fighter; he was a friend
He fought a good fight when it came to the crunch
And that's how we knew him; we called him "One Punch"
He defended his pals; he wouldn't put up with any stuff
Once known as strong and rugged and tough

Though yes, he had his failings, he had his great fall
But nothing would stop him … no, nothing at all
An accident would leave him damaged and hurt
He still would give, from his back, his own last shirt
His pride may have been wounded, his hearing impaired
In so many different ways, he still showed that he cared
He would flash that ole smile, and make everyone lighter
For he would overcome all these battles, for he was a fighter

In youth, a Pop Warner football star halfback
A wingman standing by your side, watching your back
A brother who was tough, so very tough and wild
Then an uncle so sweet, being present for a child
A fearless fighter whom no one could ever really tame
Hammering nails in high school, he would learn how to frame
Advanced classes, running track were part of his youth
Hiding out until he surrendered the transparent truth

He said it was God who choose to take his hearing away
Since he wasn't listening, messing up, and going astray

A coma for one month, then rehab consistently
Eleven years later he would have his computer degree
Finding work at the VA, he would make his life pleasant
He found himself again – humble, thoughtful and present
Even when sickness and surgery took him far far away
Friends could tell he was still in there fighting to stay
On the fateful July evening it became clear it would not be long
Even though he was isolated at times, we knew he just wanted to belong

Though he had, like we all do, a lurking shadow
He was a teammate who could lead just as soon as follow
Revealing on his terms what there was deep below
He remains, as always, our Russell Aaron Shatto
A persevering loyal warrior who would lend a friendly hand
He would take his final breath after taking a final stand
He was a fighter; he was a friend
From the beginning … until the end

THE BOY I KNEW

A prose for Jamie Jordan, a best friend growing up in Huntington Beach, on one of those neighborhood blocks we will carry in our souls forever. Born May 11, 1963. He left too soon: July 20, 2021.

Cambay Lane, across the street, a best friend zero to eleven
A buddy, experiencing life, everything from hell to heaven
Full participation, playing all out, giving our best, fully alive
All that could fit between 1963 and 1975
It was during these magic times, we lived, laughed and grew
This was Jamie Jordan … that's the boy I knew

Early, as an infant I stopped breathing, I was rescued by his mom
There was Dale, Jim, Kris, Kim, Jamie – and a handful of animals
that came along
Living next to the Fehners – Kathleen and us would dance to
the Fifth Dimension
"The Age of Aquarius" was our tune, lemon drops taking most of our attention
Calling me out to play in the morning – no knock, no words –
just bouncing a basketball
Collecting baseball cards, marbles, Slurpee cups – hey, why did he get them all?
Well, at least I got to keep the airplane made out of only three planks of wood
But wait! All the baseball cards, marbles, and Slurpee cups? Not good
Though, walking to school with the gang every day, one time I forgot my lunch
I ran home to retrieve it – Jamie the only one to wait for me out of the bunch
I loved Terry Shannon; he loved Lori Franke, the red-haired girl
At the dentist office, he'd go in the bathroom and loudly pretend to hurl
His house had a family room and UHF and one of the first color TVs
Laying around all day on a lazy Saturday – doing as we pleased
Speed Racer, Little Rascals, Dennis the Menace, Sesame Street – whatever was on
I remember he liked the Carpenters' "Top of the World"
and Helen Reddy's "Delta Dawn"

We loved the Dolphins and Dodgers, even wore the team's colors, playing catch
We could get free baseball game tickets with enough Pepsi bottle caps
Birthday parties, trick or treating, in my backyard we put on a show
Little Indian guides, Country Day, Chinger, Whitey and "Go Huffer Go"
A real and lethal bow and arrow – a Christmas gift he got
Into puddles of mud after the rain – slide, jump and flop
At his house, in the back, he had this cool tree house fort
We exploded the firecracker in our faces, the wick was just too short
Earning money for the Freedom fireworks, including the big King Kong
Putting water into my dad's gas tank – man, what a ding dong
Slicing up some upholstery and my leg with a razor, that was pretty bad
He said that was the worst whoopin' he ever got from his dad
Time would move swiftly along, yes time just flew
Jamie, from 0 – 11 … that's the boy I knew

And then there were all the sports and games, competing like a rival brother
We had to be on the same team, or we would have surely killed each other
A game of "pickle" on my lawn – the other kids would come to play
"Smear the queer" was downright violent – we could barely walk the next day
Playing basketball with his backboard … hmm, how can we clear the driveway?
Accidentally sending his mom's car to the middle of Cambay
Mother May I, Red Light Green Light, freeze tag, kick ball
Five pitch, three flies up, 4-square, tetherball
Playing "interception" with Kathy, Glenn Lappin or maybe Mark Christie
Epic games of hide and seek … where the white light pole was "free"
Games were always fair, mostly fun-spirited and never mean
Though when you lost you had to go through the "spanking machine"
All those sporting competitions – man we both wanted to win
His fight with Clay Platt was cool; he kicked him right under the chin
Jamie was fiercely loyal; he would fight anyone to protect his own
Clete, Ruben and Billy – the Cubs little league team, playing at home
Then a funeral for Ruben, buried in his uniform – so young to die
Jim Jordan, Jamie's dad, on the way there, saying: "It's OK to cry"
We were hippy longhaired kids, inseparable … until things went bad
Spitting water over my head and laughing – it made me just so mad

Then a reunion the first day of 6th grade – he came over to my house that day
I opened the door; he was always so simple – "Hey, do you want to
come outside and play?"
One sad summer his family moved – only to Irvine … not too far?
Hmm, when you're only 11 – it might as well be the Moon or a distant star
The loss of a buddy, a competitor … no one would really understand
I'd have to let him go … to become the adult man
Yet memories can keep alive what time cannot do
Nothing with ever take away – Jamie Jordan, the boy I knew
The boy I knew

The Next Time We Meet

We lost Mike Villanueva May 3, 2017. A great friend to many, a son, an uncle, a dear soul. And another reminder to never wait to share whatever there is to share.

Excited, anticipating – I long to see you again
We'll share where we're going and where we've been
We'll reminisce about the great times and all of that stuff
High fives, and high purpose – we won't get enough
It will be awesome, a treasure, a trick and a treat
This will all happen the next time we meet

Besides the good times, there may be the bad
Some of those moments of darkness we've had
The experiences of betrayal or let down or dread
Those barriers that keep us from forging ahead
I guess I'll have to share them to feel now complete
That won't be an issue … the next time we meet

The next time we meet – can it ever truly come?
The next time we meet – a task never done
The next time we meet – pushed further, further on
The next time we meet – the moment is gone

For it's true there arises a reality of "too late"
When we decide to push it off in the pursuit of the wait
The passing, the departure of a soul not meant to leave
So that all that remains is to regret and to grieve
No one is ever ready; we were not complete
I do not, now, know of the next time we meet

God willing, there will come a day – full of light and full of grace
When we're done with the treadmill and the ugly rat race
When we're finished with waiting and pushing it off
When the avoiding and hiding will finally stop

In a haven where all is resolved and all is complete
We'll join in a higher place … the next time we meet

The next time we meet – It never truly comes
The next time we meet – The future never begun
The next time we meet – The present here and now
The next time we meet – Time to surrender and to allow…

The next time we meet

I Close My Eyes

There is always too much to see when a loved one's body starts to fail them. For four years, my mother held to a physical existence after a fall made her pretty much bedridden. Years later, I had the chance to imagine something else. In this piece of prose, all it took was me closing my eyes.

I close my eyes
And my mother stands before me ... smiling, laughing, attentive
She leans in, listening to the events of the day
She makes her way to the kitchen table where she drinks her coffee and does her crossword puzzle
The newspaper is near

I close my eyes

And it's the way it's been
No different from the past
When times were simpler and there was no need for the pain or the painkillers

I close my eyes and the pain is gone
The hospital bed is back to the hospital where it belongs
The space is made clear again for the reclining chair and the Christmas tree
and the empty space for sitting on the floor
The wheelchair is no longer here

I close my eyes

And my mother is happy, and present
Laughing at a silly joke, or making one of her own
I close my eyes
And a tear of remembrance reminds me of a love that can never be erased
Or altered
By time, by space ... by pain, by a frail body that has suffered through time and space

I close my eyes
And I am there
And she is there
And we are together again in the presence
So she can rest pain-free ... and my mind can relax stress-free
And so I can ... once again ... close my eyes

POETRY PORTRAITS
GIFTS TO LOVED ONES

Over the years, I have been hired to sculpt what I have called a "Poetry Portrait" out of the sentiments of someone who wanted to gift a loved one with a customized poem.

After interviewing clients, I will take their precise words and use it to create a heartfelt message of love and appreciation. These pieces – designed with photos placed into a frame – have been called "the greatest gift I've ever received" on many occasions.

It's not the poet that is "the greatest." It is the direct and higher message that comes through loud and clear. I share some examples here, knowing that many such messages are universal.

ALWAYS

This portrait originated from the interview of Karen and Kristen Beltran, sisters wishing to gift their mother Raquel with a poem. You know how hard it is to write a poem using the word selection of 4- and 10-year-olds? My goodness. But according to the subject of the poem – a mother who reads this prose every single night – it really worked. The love behind the sentiments must make it so.

She's nice and kind and has all this fun with us
She cooks and takes us places and buys all of this stuff
We do pictures with Santa and for our Holy Communion Day
On the counter is a flowerpot and the pictures in a frame
We play outside in the back – she chases us, right by the trees
On the park swings – when we get closer, she tickles our knees
She brings snacks if we get hungry, an apple every time
Crackers, juice, applesauce … and popsicles sometimes
But there is one thing that's always; it's always for us
It's not the pictures or snacks or any of the stuff
It's nice and kind, like when we feel all snug
Yes always … what she gives us … is always a hug

And when we wake up in the morning, she makes the blankets gone
She sings "Time to wake up, time to wake up" – the morning song
She always makes us laugh; she always knows what to do
She cooks us all kinds of things – spaghetti and meatball soup
She buys us dresses, glasses, sometimes toys and shoes
At Justice, an Easter dress with flowers … in our favorite blue
When we're sad, she reads a book or gives us something to eat
Twix, Snickers, mints, or an ice cream treat
When we're sick, she won't work but will stay at home
And put on "Frozen," cartoons, Barbie, Caillou – so we're never alone
She took us on vacation to the Grand Canyon – no school!
We stayed at three hotels, moved each day – so cool!

She got us gifts to remember the trip – dream catchers, toys and rocks
Lots of pictures of memories, flowers and lollipops
She took us to Rosarito where we could ride a horse and not fall
She was scared, me too … until I got on and I felt tall
On the beach, a knee got an owie, and she didn't get mad
She just yelled, "I have to go to the car and get the medical bag"
A decorated rock, at home she put eyes on it – looky!
She even helped us name the new pet – Cookie!
And then … when the day is over and it's time to go to bed
It's time to get under the covers … and then be tickled instead
She reads too – "Hungry Caterpillar" and "The Color of my Own"
It's about a lizard that also wants to have its own color in its own home
She then tells us there will be no bites from the bad bed bug
And then it's here, when she always … always gives us a hug

She is kind, silly and loud … and really, really funny
She asks us if we want to be tickled on the back or the tummy
She calls her class "green chickens" right from the start
She calls me "Punchis" … and she calls me "Little Heart"
We just want to tell her we love to stay with her, and enjoy being near
She really makes us laugh a lot; she gives us nothing to fear
The thing we really love about her is she's kind and always tries to make
people glad
She doesn't like to see people upset; she doesn't want to see anyone sad
All that she gives us is really great; it's all of these things
But the best thing she gives us is bigger than anything
She makes us feel as snug as a bug in a rug
Always … what she gives us … is always a hug

ON POINT

Here is a Poetry Portrait written for someone I had not met. Research would have to come through the Internet and a friend of a friend. This was dedicated to Nicole Gee, a soldier lost so tragically and too soon.

Remaining behind, post withdrawal, taking the hard and strong stand
Hamid Karzai International Airport – Kabul, Afghanistan
From Sacramento, married, a young marine, all of 23
August 26, terrorist suicide attack, taken, Nicole L. Gee
Six days prior, pictures, loving her job … then the report came along
"There was an explosion. And just like that … she's gone"
One of thirteen, lost in a mere moment, lost in a flash
Identification, a flight, a casket draped with the American flag
Flying home to Roseville, where family awaits a final farewell
Honor, legacy, commitment, care … she did her job so well
Services and speeches, tears and tributes, so many memories to anoint
Nicole on guard, on her game, on her post … always on point

In her role, everything must run smooth, everything must be set
Handling the logistics – ensuring everyone's needs get met
Succeeding at her mission, so the larger operation would not fail
A caregiver – with clear mind, open heart, and attention to detail
Promoted to sergeant in August, ground electronics transmissions
Combat Logistics Battalion 24, maintenance systems
Her reliable nature, her carefulness, her clarity – this, the best defense
The invisible, behind-the-scenes impact … all of it immense
Social media posts, a job in progress, a job worthwhile – yes, a positive word
Ushering other souls to safety, "escorting evacuees onto the bird"
She was good at what she did, everything taken care of, where it needed to be
Caring about the lives of others … marine sergeant Nicole L. Gee
A proud and honored military member, serving a country, saving the day
Out there faithfully holding the line, out there in harm's way

No matter the locale, she'd dot the I's, cross the T's and clearly case the joint
A marine on guard, on her post, on the front lines … always on point

And then there is Nicole, humble, what you get is what you see
Beyond the weapons, the tasks, the boots, and the battle fatigues
A marine's marine, passionate and motivated, a light in a dark world
"I love my job," she posted … while cradling an infant Afghan girl
Holding high an oath to country and a community she held dear
Determination and fearlessness fueled a passion for career
"A hometown hero," married to Jarod, committed to her work
Her sister would say, "We will be forever changed and hurt"
A casualty of violence, a tale no one would ever want to tell
Honor, legacy, commitment, care … she lived her life so well
In some higher world of beauty, may all fallen soldiers find peaceful home
She wasn't just one of 13, or one in a million, but rather one of our own
For now, a new position, a new mission, one that only God shall appoint
Nicole L. Gee – forever in our hearts and prayers, forever out there … on point

THE MOST IMPORTANT THING IN MY WORLD

A Valentine's Day love poem for a pet owner, from a pet. How can that be, you ask? This came through the eyes of Jonah for Wendy Prestera, courtesy of an interview with Wendy's husband Marc Prestera. Did you follow that? I just sculpted the words into a rhyme, not routinely done by the common canine.

You call me J-Man, Jonah-Balona, Doghead and Bublet
Jonsey, Goof-ball, Silly Dog, Silly Boy and Puplet
No matter the name, it would be just the same
For in the end, all that matters … is that you came
I was in doggie prison for nine months before you came to call
Kiwi and Einstein didn't exactly welcome me with open paws
But you rescued me, took me in, even though you had your own pains
And though you didn't really like it, you would even walk me in the rain
Living the crate life wasn't the great life, but we'd become "a dog and his girl"
Indeed, you were the most important thing in my world

You're like me: tall, with long legs, and certain skip to your step
I'm so excited to spend time with you, I jump up towards your neck
You're awesome, I am your dog, I am yours … and you are mine
You walk me every morning and night – no matter rain or shine
You feed me every day, and every two weeks I get a bath
It doesn't matter that I sit in the car … I know you're coming back
We go everywhere: to Alabama, Northern Cal, or even just to the store
You take me on hikes with your friends – with legs both two and four
The beach, the water, Dogtopia, the big field with coyotes I can chase
And every morning and after work, I get to snuggle up to your face
In the bed we can cuddle, both of us in a ball we can curl
You have become the most important thing in my world

I know you get upset when I chase bunnies, or eat junk food off the ground
Or when I try to eat the squirrels that tend to run around

I just can't help myself … sorry … I do what I like to do
It has nothing to do with how much I admire and appreciate you
Always caring about me, you take me to the vet when I get sick
When I hurt my knee, you took me to rehab so my knee could get fixed
When I almost died … you did everything in the world that you could do
Saying goodbye to Kiwi and Einstein – yeah, I miss them too

You love me, talk to me, cry with me, I'm always here for you
I especially like when you're cooking and you let me sample the food
Let's continue to be the best of friends – you, me and Marc
I'll always want to greet you with a wagging tail and an "I love you" bark
Thank you for being my Valentine, and for all those nicknames
For in the end … all that matters … is that you came
The story of Wendy and me – a story of a dog and his girl
Yes, you are the most important thing in my world
The most important thing in my world

THESE MAKE THE MAN

*This was written in 2014 for Father's Day, a gift from Willy and Eric Holt after
I interviewed both of these sons and put into prose their sentiments about
a dad named Bill. Pictured here at left on his wedding day.*

This is a prose for a dad, a close and caring one
A man born in Halfway, Missouri in 1931
He was born in a barn, now that's been the line
His grandfather delivered him right on time
The family came to San Diego – in a home of endless summer
Making sure to land a job, his own father said, "Yeah … I'm a plumber"
Married two years out of high school, in the month of September
He would create a life of memories that we shall remember
Drafted into the army, he did what he had to do
So many jobs – piano mover, navy supply, data processing – to name a few
He would climb the ladder, moving higher and ever higher
San Diego Unified made him operations supervisor
But these are simply the jobs and the necessary tasks at hand
They do not make a father; they do not make a man

For this man possesses qualities so precious and pure
Responsible, present and thorough – he wants to make sure
Supportive – he always encourages us to do well
He has lived a life to show … and not to tell
A living example teaching how a man can be his best
He was the rock the whole time, passing every single test
Not pressuring or forcing, he didn't yell when things went wrong
In charge of his emotions, he's been even keel all along
Easygoing and calm – he has that simple and steady smile
With visitors – it's "come on and in and stay awhile"
His upbeat nature – he's almost always in a good mood
He doesn't complain – he's got that steady attitude
A researcher before purchase, he is precise and attentive
Creating anything, he's meticulous to the point of anal-retentive
Teaching right from wrong, a good work ethic and how to be kind
Without hesitation, willing to help another, so generous with time
A natural teacher, he exposes us to all things worth seeing
Always involved, always concerned about our wellbeing

Now, as we look over our shoulder, we peer into yonder year
We find a host of memories of a father so dear…

Riding down the Colorado River with a raft and no fear
Boy scouts, football and baseball – he didn't let work interfere
Looking up into the bleachers we would simply know
There he'd be, straight from work, in his work clothes
For square dancing, in the outfit duds he was all dressed up
Wearing cool plaid Pendleton shirts, he'd roll the sleeves up
In the roller derby, our dragster never won but looked the best
Willy somehow won a blue ribbon for the cake contest
A trip to Europe, seeing Germany, Netherlands, Austria, Italy and the Swiss
On a trip to Oregon, he would teach us how to fish
Before the bridge, we went to Coronado at the Harbor Ferry's pace
Taking us to many museums – from Munich to Salt Mines to Aerospace

Washing and waxing his car until it was looking super-duper clean
To see our grades early, he could slow down the report card machine
Drawing numbers on Willy's game flags, he would take forever
To ensure Eric wasn't losing it, they took a meditation class together
Doing it all without grievance or grumble,
though his legs and back would hurt
He helped granddaughters build missions, doing so much of the work
Then there is the lineage, the grand tradition of legacy
Marissa, Alex, Lauren, Arielle, Hannah, Hudson and Timothy
It's what lay beyond memories, behind timepieces and the fine grains of sand
This is what makes a father; this is what makes a man
This is what makes a man

So now we say thank you, you've given a lifetime for us
For Willy ... You helped me get sober; that helped me so very much
You showed me how a man must provide for his family
Doing the right thing, without complaint, but with pure humility
Thank you for being a good example, for giving us everything
For being – in our house – the mature and masculine king
For Eric ... You show me how to do the right thing and do it all the time
Your happiness, humor and work ethic has today become mine
Your lessons will endure through life's challenges and tests
Thank you for caring enough about us and our success
For being a role model, rather than judging and preaching
So that we may all live a good life through your true teaching

We share this here for you, so caring and so close
You are the one we celebrate; your guidance has meant the most
We trust you can receive this; we hope you understand
You taught us how to be a father ... you taught us to be a man

When I See My Mom, I Smile

A poetry prose written for the mother of a friend Rick. He teared up during the interview. "Oh, you got me again, Ellis!" Truthfully, I think what got him emotional was the memories and the momma.

Adorable and sweet – with her, hearts are lifted
So considerate of others, she keeps you in mind
High energy, high on life – super high-spirited
Caring and bubbly … and one of a kind
Meticulous with her life – organized and clean
Everything in order in her home
Dust-free pictures and well-placed figurines
As host and housekeeper, she looks after her own
I see her at family events; it's always the same
It's what I've come to expect, and what I seek
She'll jaunt over, claiming "Sonbun" my name
Big smile, open arms and a kiss on the cheek

When I see my mom – I see a relationship amazing
When I see my mom – I know a connection never fading
When I see my mom – It's "come on in, and stay awhile"
When I see my mom – I smile, I smile

She was a coal miner's daughter
They didn't have much to spare
She learned how to stretch a dollar
She covered us with her care
She would stay home for us kids
Until I was junior in high school
Even when I didn't follow the rules
She somehow kept her cool
Sometimes we'd have breakfast for dinner
I never knew we didn't have much

Through Summer, Fall, Spring and Winter
There was always, always enough

Sending us to private school, that was always a given
I had what I needed when the need arose
Raising us mainly while Dad made the living
Sewing, washing, spraying, and pressing our clothes
Keeping a tight budget, she taught us to treasure
She took care of the family, feeding us well
Embracing the value, measure by measure
The love was present, we always could tell
And her cooking, oh yeah, amazing
A cook who could make just about anything
Didn't matter if I was scarfing or if I was grazing
I'd have to devour almost everything
Mouth-watering dumpling soup, stuffed cabbage golumpki
And mini meatloaf burgers also known as wimpys
And scalpies, ziti, plotskies, and shrimp scampi
Then the most wonderful of cheese and macaroni
Made with tomato soup and bits – American and cheddar
It was awesome and yet also chunky odd
Life at the dinner table couldn't get much better
You'd try it and think ... "Oh my God!"

When I see my mom – I see a relationship amazing
When I see my mom – I know a connection never fading
When I see my mom – It's "come on in, and stay awhile"
When I see my mom – I smile, I smile

Memories appear, come and go, rise and fall
I had bronchitis and fevers, a sickly kid
Though I always felt safe, not lacking at all
Just because of a mother who would do what she did
Yes, I struggled in class, didn't apply as I should
I'd sit in my room and think on why I was there
An underachiever who didn't always achieve what I could

Sad to put her through that; I now know it wasn't fair
She never gave up on me, never disconnected or quit
Though times got dicey, problematic and sticky
I'm so grateful her support never budged one bit
So that a "Richard" could always be known as her "Ricky"
Five decades of commitment through any rough spot
Kelly Ann – or KellBell – a sister for me
There was Uncle Frank, Uncle Lenny, Chuchie Rini, Chuchie Dot
Dinner hangouts Don Pepes and Fernandez III
Bermuda trips, Jersey City, Central Avenue
To Glenwood in the Poconos in our car
A 50th anniversary Bahamas cruise
Laughing as she scooted to get closer to the bar

Lessons learned, teaching me to respect everyone
And the difference between what is right and what is wrong
And when everything is said and everything is done …
Stands her pride in us all and how we've come along
It's her unconditional acceptance that I truly adore
So proud of a mom on this special Mother's Day
Embracing the past and also what's in store
Feeling the love … every step of the way

When I see my mom – I feel unconditional care
When I see my mom – I know her love will be there
When I see my mom – I'm happy she let me stay longer than "awhile"
When I see my mom – I smile, I smile

Epilogue

Looking Down the Road

After the journey is complete and the family and loved ones are embraced, we are left here: at the end of the road … looking further down the path.

The road ahead, like life experiences and the foundation of love beneath it all, just goes on and on and on …

THE WORLD IS REALLY PRETTY RIGHT NOW

This poem feels like it would fit into a chapter that completes a journey. I don't even recall me being on a train writing this, but it sure paints a nice picture of a world almost passed by.

The Sun sets as the tracks roll beneath me
I peer through a window revealing the sand and the sea
Then I rest again, eyes closed, sitting silently in my seat
Stillness, I make my exit as the journey is complete
Home I walk the streets, the glowing bulbs illuminate trees
I fall into myself, I fall into bliss, I fall to my knees
Amazed, the universal flow, all hail, please take a bow
The world is really pretty right now

A world really pretty – reminding us of the depth
Knowing the times we have laughed and the times we have wept
Knowing of our sorrow – all that we have lost
Knowing the consequences of injury, all at a cost
Recognizing our purity and beauty beneath it all
Recognizing our mother's and father's voice – an echo down the hall
Remembering our childhood nickname – ah, the source of joy
Remembering when we were simply ... a girl ... a boy
All the wonderment and innocence that the Universe will allow
The world is really pretty right now

It's quiet and still and shimmering in the fading light
Giving way to a deeper stillness that is the night
Yet the darkness does not remain or stay for very long
It ushers in another tomorrow, right where we belong
Sometimes hard to know, this dance of righteous divinity
I open wide my eyes in order to see all there is to see

And I stand astonished, mouth agape, in the wonder and the wow
The world is really pretty right now
So pretty
Right now
Now
Now

I've Admired You from a Distance

For this poem, I imagined spirit guides or God looking upon this creation – you and I – and carrying the sort of admiration that only the Divine could offer.

So far, so far away
I look upon you, with grace, every day
A higher self, a higher mind, a higher being
You may not know the truth that I am seeing
Without the judgment of a divisive right or wrong
The place you stand is where you belong
Though at times lost, you wander alone in the dark
Before, eventually, you get the horse before the cart
Alas the gift: your very presence, your very existence
Just so you know – I've admired you from a distance

The list of struggles and stressors are real
Those who search for the sustenance of a simple meal
Those who have no shelter, no room, no home, no bed
Those who battle inner demons in their own head
You who falter on promises to stop the latest addiction
You who get bad news of the latest medical affliction
You who fall prey to the latest government sponsored racket
You who work hard for money lost in your tax bracket
In the end, you need not struggle with any offense or defense
For little did you know – I've admired you from a distance

Those who cheat another for no other reason but because they can
Those who meet their mirror – the karma they come to understand
Those who believe they have fallen, blindly, too far
Alas, those who have forgotten who they are
Every hair on your head, everything will be held to account
While every barrier, challenge and mountain you shall surmount

With each resistance met, with a soul's endless persistence
No, not so far, not so far away – your very existence
Dissolution discarded, unity embraced, within this very instance
I will admire you eternally – knowing there is no distance

SOMEONE SOMEWHERE SMILES

I know I write for various reasons. One of the major reasons is you and your smile.

What do I want when I want it?
What do I want when I do what I do?
What is my desire when the creative sparks hit
When my writing decides to come on through
It may take an anguishing writer's block
It may take the first step of 1000 miles
Yet I realize nothing could ever make me stop
Until the time ... someone somewhere smiles

If it's not a joke or a poke or a silly gag
Then it's a poem, an article, some piece of prose
Turning an audience from the upset, and the sad
To lift them to a place the archangel knows
Yes, it is that sense of joy that I am after
To stir up some happiness, lightness and glee
A bonus would be some falling-on-the-floor laughter
Or even someone having to hold back their pee
Or even a snicker, a snort or perhaps just a grin
This would satisfy a writer who pours over his art
That would be my championship trophy in a big-time win
Readers who read my words and then land directly into their heart

So I shall carry on, sometimes early morn or late into the night
Refining the lines, perfecting the meter
Making sure I write what is right
And playing the game of finders keepers
I shall keep what works and archive it into forever
No matter the format, the medium or the styles
These words shall always keep us together
Where, on into eternity, someone somewhere smiles

ONLY 10 MINUTES WITH YOU

As part of a #justwrite31 challenge in which I would write daily for all 31 days of the month, I realized I only had 10 minutes left of the day before my writing deadline was upon me. So, this came through swiftly. Maybe I can call it #justwrite10minutes — especially if that is the window of time I have with you this day.

If I only had 10 minutes to spend with you
What would I say; what would I do?
Would I spit out a ton of rapid thoughts and emotion
Or would I move towards you in effortless slow-motion
And look deeply in your eyes, rekindling a love
Would I reveal what our relationship was made of
Or maybe clear up any misunderstandings or spite
Those barriers that block the miracle that is life

What would I say or do Mom?
We pretty much always got along
I'd want to know more about you, your inner world
The "you" who was "you" when you were a little girl

What would I say or do Dad?
Engaging and enlivening were the times we had
I may find out what you know now of 911 and JFK
But most of all, I'd want to know if you are OK

What would I say or do Miss Hennessy dear?
You were the cherry on top, that is clear
I would simply want to grab a chew toy and play
And do with you what I miss now every day

For all the times I've said goodbye
I want to awaken to the connections that will never die
So now, I endeavor to fill my heart with loved ones in gratitude
As if I only had 10 minutes to spend with you ...

YOUR SKY

*A final analogy and a final symbol of the eternal. A yoga teacher recently made
a remark about reaching upwards during the exercise practice. She didn't say,
"reach towards the ceiling" but rather "reach towards your sky." I quite liked that.
I imagined how empowering it would be to reclaim the fact that
we choose our life here.*

Not your childhood, not your choice
Not your beliefs, not your voice
Sent to school to learn as they believe
Following their directions and their needs
But it's yours to take back … reclaim, recover
It's your life to, once again, create and discover
As you lay down on grass, without a question why
You fall into the exalted and your very own sky

It's your sky – you peer into a world of forever
It's your sky – you float upwards on a feather

Your sky – you're the one who calls in rain and clouds
Your sky – you're the one who tears it apart with doubts
Your sky – a blank canvas with infinity as a backdrop
Your sky – you alone can make the thunder and rain stop

No longer holding chains from the past, you can start anew
You can paint in all colors magenta, indigo, green and blue
You can take a stand for who you are beyond preconceived beliefs
You can recall your playful and joyful spirit that resides underneath
This is your day, this is your time, this is the moment to fly
It's your life, it's your soul's journey, it is your sky

Your sky – no need to struggle or try
No longer the dread of barely getting by
Your sky – ascend into the realm near the rays of the sun
Your time, your life – forever in this moment begun
There is that which was never born and never will die
It's found in your heart and soul; it's found in your sky

Your sky
Your sky

ACKNOWLEDGMENTS

My wife Jennifer - with an eternal "kiss, kiss, kiss"
Our Akita girl Hennessy
Olga Singer of SimplyTwo Design for her wonderful book design
Willy Holt for all the years of support
Dylan Stewart and his #justwrite challenge

INSPIRATIONS:

My agitating and faithful muse
Cody and Grace Mendoza - along with Abigail and Allison
Emmett and Amy Kellogg - along with Elijah, Hannah and Shiloh
Karen Pearlman and her Chloe
Wendy and Marc Prestera along with Jonah
Roger and his Daisy
Jorge Beltran along with Raquel, Karen and Kristen
Attila Tota and his dear wife Lisa Kalison-Tota
Dawn and Sammie
Rick Wright and his momma
Bryce and Marci
Janet and Fred Lundquist
Russell Shatto
Jamie Jordan
Mike Villanueva
The dynamic trio - Audra, Michael and Consuelo
And Mom and Dad and Mary Lynn and Kathy

About the Author

James Anthony Ellis is an award-winning playwright, journalist, poet, and filmmaker who creates videos, books, theater, and productions that bring understanding to "what's really going on" in our society. His first book, "Starting Point: A Guide to Metaphysics, the Golden Time and Love," was initially published in 1989. Other books include "Morning Musings," "Huh?: The Joys, Sorrows and Comic Relief of Miscommunication," "Life Traveler," "Tears," "Breadcrumbs," "The Honor Book" and "Preparing for the Best: A Guide to Global Changes for the Earth, The Society and You."

Owner of Legacy Productions since 2000, Ellis has produced twenty plays, 100+ film/video productions and countless articles and columns. In 2011, he filmed and produced the highly acclaimed "Indoctrinated: The Grooming of our Children into Prostitution," to bring awareness to our prostituted youth problem. In 2019, Ellis filmed and produced the short documentary "Keeping the Peace: Mental and Emotional Wellness for our Law Enforcement," which garnered national attention from police agencies in 36 states.

Since 1998, Ellis has been in leadership within MDI, an international men's organization, including the role as Division Coordinator of the San Diego Men's Division, International VP of Media, and Legacy Magazine editor. A proponent of equality and liberty everywhere, he has spent time focused on issues facing males through the "Boys to Men" nonprofit mentoring organization as well as the Coalition to Create a White House Council on Boys and Men, led by best-selling author Dr. Warren Farrell.

Regarding his poetry, to put it succinctly, James Anthony Ellis likes rhyming stuff, especially if it can inspire others in some positive way.

He can be reached at www.LegacyProductions.org.